To Hazard All

A GUIDE TO THE MARYLAND CAMPAIGN, 1862

by Robert Orrison and Kevin R. Pawlak

EMERGING CIVIL WAR SERIES

Chris Mackowski, series editor
Chris Kolakowski, chief historian

The Emerging Civil War Series

offers compelling, easy-to-read overviews of some of the Civil War's most important battles and stories.

Recipient of the Army Historical Foundation's Lieutenant General Richard G. Trefry Award for contributions to the literature on the history of the U.S. Army

Also part of the Emerging Civil War Series:

Determined to Stand and Fight: The Battle of Monocacy, July 9, 1864
   by Ryan T. Quint

The Last Road North: A Guide to the Gettysburg Campaign, 1863
   by Robert Orrison and Dan Welch

No Turning Back: A Guide to the 1864 Overland Campaign, from the Wilderness to Cold Harbor, May 4 - June 13, 1864
   by Robert M. Dunkerly, Donald C. Pfanz, and David R. Ruth

Simply Murder: The Battle of Fredericksburg, December 13, 1862
   by Chris Mackowski and Kristopher D. White

That Field of Blood: The Battle of Antietam, September 17, 1862
   by Daniel J. Vermilya

A Want of Vigilance: The Bristoe Station Campaign, October 9-19, 1863
   by Bill Backus and Robert Orrison

For a complete list of titles in the Emerging Civil War Series, visit www.emergingcivilwar.com.

Also by Kevin R. Pawlak:
Shepherdstown in the Civil War: One Vast Confederate Hospital (History Press, 2015)

To Hazard All

A GUIDE TO THE MARYLAND CAMPAIGN, 1862

by Robert Orrison and Kevin R. Pawlak

EMERGING CIVIL WAR SERIES

SB
Savas Beatie
California

First edition, first printing

ISBN-13 (paperback): 978-1-61121-409-3
ISBN-13 (ebook): 978-1-61121-410-9

Library of Congress Cataloging-in-Publication Data

Names: Orrison, Robert, author. | Pawlak, Kevin R., author.
Title: To hazard all : a guide to the Maryland Campaign, 1862 / by Robert Orrison and Kevin Pawlak.
Other titles: Guide to the Maryland Campaign, 1862
Description: El Dorado Hills, California : Savas Beatie LLC, [2018]
Identifiers: LCCN 2018030381| ISBN 9781611214093 (pbk : alk. paper) | ISBN 9781611214109 (ebk)
Subjects: LCSH: Maryland Campaign, 1862. | Maryland--History--Civil War, 1861-1865--Guidebooks.
Classification: LCC E474.61 .O77 2018 | DDC 975.2/03--dc23
LC record available at https://lccn.loc.gov/2018030381

SB

Published by
Savas Beatie LLC
989 Governor Drive, Suite 102
El Dorado Hills, California 95762
Phone: 916-941-6896
Email: sales@savasbeatie.com
Web: www.savasbeatie.com

Savas Beatie titles are available at special discounts for bulk purchases in the United States by corporations, institutions, and other organizations. For more details, please contact Special Sales, P.O. Box 4527, El Dorado Hills, CA 95762, or you may e-mail us at sales@savasbeatie.com, or visit our website at www.savasbeatie.com for additional information.

MIX
Paper from
responsible sources
FSC
www.fsc.org   FSC® C011935

Rob: *Dedicated to the memory of a great historian, teacher, and mentor, Dr. Joseph Harsh, leader of the "Harsh Brigade."*

Kevin: *To my family–my wife, my parents, and my brothers and sisters*

Table of Contents

* * *

List of Maps

Maps by Hal Jespersen

Acknowledgments

PHOTO CREDITS: Appleton's Cyclopaedia of American Biography (acab); *Battles and Leaders of the Civil War* (b&l); *A Centennial Biographical History of Richland County, Ohio* (cbhrco); Daniel Davis (dd); Gilder Lehrman Institute of American History (gliah); *Harper's Weekly* (hw); *History of the Independent Loudoun Virginia Rangers* (lvar); *Illustrated London News* (iln); Loudoun Museum (lm); Library of Congress (loc); Library of Virginia (lva); *Lossing's Illustrated History of the United States* (lihus); Chris Mackowski (cm); National Archives and Records Administration (nara); Robert Orrison (ro); Kevin Pawlak (kp); *The Photographic History of the Civil War* (phcw); Richard Gillespie, Mosby Heritage Area Association (rgmhaa); Wikipedia (w)

First, we would like to thank Chris Mackowski for being the force behind the Emerging Civil War project. Thank you to Ted Savas and the staff at Savas Beatie for the opportunity to add our part to the scholarship on the Maryland Campaign. Hal Jespersen flexibly worked with our constant map updates and edits; we think readers will appreciate Hal's attention to detail.

As we began this project, we did not intend to retell the story of the Maryland Campaign of 1862. Already there are many great books by good friends of ours on this campaign. We wanted this book to work in conjunction with the other studies on the Maryland Campaign. You can read about the events of late summer 1862, then go see these sites, driving and walking the routes of march. To see the battle sites enhances one's understanding of these events. In addition, we wanted to promote preservation and remembrance of the men and women on both sides who sacrificed so much.

To ensure we created a comprehensive study-tour of the campaign, we relied on several people to assist us. Tom Clemens, Kate Bitely, Jim Rosebrock, Dan Welch, Ed Wenzel, and ECW Chief Historian Chris Kolakowski all reviewed the manuscript and maps to make this work better with their comments and suggestions. Dan Vermilya graciously shared his maps and insight with us. Friend and Civil War Trails Executive Director Drew Gruber helped make sure all of our tour stops were up to date with the latest Civil War Trails signage. We wanted to ensure our book was a good companion piece to the popular Civil War Trails program.

If we failed to mention anyone, the fault is all ours, as we know this project was the product of many people not mentioned above.

Rob:

In everything I do, my family plays a crucial role. I would not be able to go out on research trips or spend hours in the library if I did not have my family. I have to thank my two young sons for constantly distracting me when working on this project. Although forcing me to stay up late to complete this project, they always remind me of what is important. They add perspective as I think about the thousands of sons and daughters who never saw their fathers again because of a bloody civil war.

Co-author Kevin Pawlak has opened my eyes to so many facets of the Maryland Campaign that I never knew before. I have enjoyed our bantering about McClellan. Kevin is a top-rate historian and interpreter and an expert on everything Maryland 1862.

Finally, I have to think the late Dr. Joseph Harsh. I was fortunate to study under him for my graduate degree at George Mason University, and many trips to the Antietam battlefield with Dr. Harsh sparked my interest in the Maryland Campaign. He was one of the best, and the world of Civil War history hasn't been the same since his passing.

Kevin:

Many books have one or two names on the cover, but there are always many more people who contribute to the publication of a book, as is the case with this guide. First, I want to thank my co-author Rob Orrison for approaching me about the project and asking me to be a part of it. Without my companions, the Antietam battlefield guides, many questions I had about the campaign might have gone unanswered. Few know the campaign and battle of Antietam better than this exceptional group of historians. I would like to especially thank Steve Stotelmyer for his assistance in locating the Reno Oak tree.

Any book requires time and commitment, which I would not have been able to adequately give to this project had it not been for my flexible and understanding wife, Kristen. In fact, I want to thank my whole family, to whom I dedicate this book—my wife, Kristen; my parents, Jerome and Teresa; and my siblings, Rion, Joseph, and Gabriella. You always tell me to forge my own path and be myself, for which I am eternally grateful.

For the Emerging Civil War Series

Theodore P. Savas, *publisher*
Chris Mackowski, *series editor*
Chris Kolakowski, *chief historian*
Sarah Keeney, *editorial consultant*
Kristopher D. White, *emeritus editor*

Maps by Hal Jespersen
Design and layout by Tara Hatmaker

MARYLAND CAMPAIGN—The lead elements of the Army of Northern Virginia began crossing the Potomac River into Maryland on September 4, 1862. The Army of the Potomac began its pursuit out of Washington the same day. Both armies marched through Frederick, Maryland, to battles at Harpers Ferry, South Mountain, Antietam, and Shepherdstown before the campaign ended just over two weeks after it began.

Touring the Battlefields

The Maryland Campaign of 1862 was multi-faceted and wide ranging geographically. This book attempts to take the reader in the footsteps of both the Federal and Confederate troops as they made their way north from Virginia into Maryland and back into Virginia. The book is divided into five tour routes: Lee Moves North, McClellan Responds, Battle of Harpers Ferry, Battle of South Mountain, and Return to Virginia.

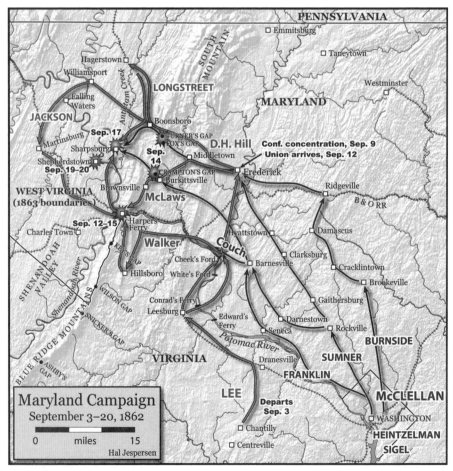

Maryland Campaign
September 3–20, 1862

0   miles   15

Hal Jespersen

Many of the sites are part of the popular Civil War Trails program and have accessible interpretive markers. The Civil War Trails guide brochure "Antietam Campaign: Lee Invades Maryland" is a helpful accessory since many of the sites are included in this book. For more information on Civil War Trails, visit www.civilwartrails.org.

Although this guide book will follow the general route of the armies, a few side trips and optional stops exist, so please be sure to consult the written directions to each stop. GPS coordinates are also provided for each stop. This book serves as a general guide for sites in the 1862 Maryland Campaign. We have no illusions about covering every site and route in September-November 1862, but we think this book will introduce people to some unique and lesser-known sites.

Be aware that the routes to Sharpsburg, Maryland, are approximately 120 miles and the return to Virginia approximately 95 miles. The distances can vary depending on which routes the traveler chooses to follow and any side trips explored. At a few locations, the tour routes may intersect each other, and in some cases, the tour visits a site twice. The armies marched in separate and far flung columns, and therefore, the tour routes will crisscross often. Many of the locations can also be further investigated at individual battlefield sites or museums. Take some time to enjoy everything the locations offer. We also encourage supporting the work to preserve the story of the Maryland Campaign of 1862.

In some instances, this tour will pass historic properties that are privately owned. Please respect the owners' privacy: do not trespass.

As much as possible, the tour routes will follow the actual roads that the armies took in 1862. Keep in mind that some roads are rural routes, and others may have heavy traffic. At times, the routes drive through neighborhoods and towns. Please follow all speed limits and park only in areas that are both safe and legal. Most of all, enjoy your tour!

Civil War Trails is a six-state tourism program connecting hundreds of Civil War sites, parks, and museums. Many of the stops in this guide are Civil War Trails locations. (ro)

"Everything seems to indicate that [the Confederates] intend to hazard all upon the issue of the coming battle."

–*George McClellan to Henry Halleck, September 11, 1862*

Prelude to the Campaign

"The present seems to be the most propitious time since the commencement of the war for the Confederate Army to enter Maryland." With this sentence, Confederate Gen. Robert E. Lee began a letter to Confederate President Jefferson Davis about his intentions to move his army northward into Maryland. Writing from his camp in Dranesville, Virginia, on September 3, 1862, Lee was simply informing Davis of what he was going to do, not necessarily seeking authorization or permission for his plans. Thus, the Maryland Campaign of 1862 began, but its origins go further back than Dranesville that fall; they began earlier that spring.

With the wounding of Confederate Gen. Joseph Johnston at the battle of Seven Pines on June 1, 1862, Robert E. Lee ascended to command of the Confederate army around Richmond. The Confederate government recruited nearly 90,000 men to defend its capital from the Army of the Potomac under Gen. George B. McClellan. McClellan had spent the winter of 1861-1862 creating the most powerful military force in the western hemisphere. With nearly 120,000 men, McClellan planned to besiege the Confederate capital, but the aggressive

The 5th Battery, Maine Light Artillery played a crucial role in delaying the Confederate onslaught on the afternoon of August 30 along Chinn Ridge. Their stubborn defense bought time for Maj. Gen. John Pope to build a defense on nearby Henry Hill, but at the cost of losing four of their five guns. (ro)

By August, Confederate Gen. Robert E. Lee had come a long way from the days of June when his men called him "King of Spades." His aggressive nature led to nearly two months of constant campaigning and fighting. (loc)

Lee denied the Union force the opportunity to succeed. In a series of bloody assaults called the "Seven Days' Campaign," Lee pushed a hesitant McClellan from the gates of Richmond back to Westover, nearly thirty miles east of Richmond. Here, McClellan claimed Lee's army had superior numbers and an attack against it would not succeed without resupply and reinforcement.

McClellan's movement on Richmond had been planned as part of a coordinated effort with a newly formed Federal force called the Army of Virginia under Maj. Gen. John Pope. This 50,000-man force consisted of several small armies that had engaged Thomas "Stonewall" Jackson in the Shenandoah Valley earlier that spring and summer. President Abraham Lincoln's strategic vision for the Federal advance on Richmond planned for the Army of the Potomac to attack from the east while the Army of Virginia engaged from the north. Unfortunately, cautiousness, miscommunication and mistrust between Pope

The battle of Seven Pines, fought on May 31-June 1, 1862, was Confederate Gen. Joseph Johnston's attempt to dislodge the Army of the Potomac from the gates of Richmond. Confused orders and mismanagement led to a bloody stalemate. The battle ended with Johnston wounded and Robert E. Lee in command of the Confederate army around Richmond. (loc)

and McClellan led to failure. By the time Pope arrived in Culpeper, Virginia, McClellan had already started moving away from Richmond.

Outside of Virginia, events in the west and in Europe encouraged Confederate leaders. Although many now argue that intervention by Great Britain and France in support of the South was a long shot, in 1862, the Confederate high command hoped for that intervention. British political leaders specifically judged the Confederacy nearly "dead" by spring of 1862, but Lee's string of stunning victories changed their attitude. Parliament and the Cabinet began discussing measures to facilitate mediation between the North and the South. Looking back now, it seems that a victory on northern soil could have moved the discussion further along. Sadly, for Jefferson Davis, the events that played out in Maryland ended the greatest chance of European intervention.

In the western theater, Confederate forces under Gen. Braxton Bragg and Gen. Kirby Smith were moving northward into Kentucky. Despite slow communication, Lee knew of

The Virginia State Capitol was designed by Thomas Jefferson and completed in 1788. By July 1861, the Virginia General Assembly began to share the building with the Confederate Congress. The building became a symbol of the Confederacy and Southern defiance. (loc)

Maj. General Thomas "Stonewall" Jackson earned a famous reputation by the summer of 1862. He first earned his name at the battle of First Manassas, then earned the respect of Federal leadership though his famous Shenandoah Valley Campaign. The defeat of Jackson was a prize that consumed John Pope. (loc)

Confederate Gen. Braxton Bragg became one of the most controversial characters of the Civil War. Trusted by Jefferson Davis, Bragg alienated nearly every other Confederate leader. In the summer of 1862, Bragg played a major role in Confederate strategy as he took his army northward into Kentucky. (loc)

Maj. Gen. George B. McClellan was the quintessential military man. A graduate of West Point, engineer, and military attaché during the Crimean War, McClellan had all the qualities of a military leader. He was well respected by his men, but constantly argued with his political leaders in Washington. (loc)

the plans in Kentucky and hoped to press the Federals on all fronts. Lee also knew that mid-term Congressional elections approached in the fall. The string of defeats in the east were beginning to wear down Northern morale, or at least Lee thought so. A victory in Maryland or Pennsylvania could go a long way, effecting change in political leadership of the United States with the possibility for peace.

Finally, Lee had the Federals in Virginia on the ropes. After one of Lee's most complete victories at the battle of Second Manassas, Pope led the battered Federal army back to Washington, DC, opening the door for McClellan's return to the forefront. All of these thoughts crowded Lee's mind as he assessed the situation on September 3. Many historians, such as the late Joseph Harsh, argued that Lee's movement northward was just another turning movement of the many turning movements that Lee had made that summer. This time, though, it brought him onto the doorstep of the Federal home front, offering the possibility of Confederate success. As the Maryland Campaign stepped off, Lee made two crucial mistakes. He overestimated his own men, who had been fighting and marching continually since June, and he underestimated his opponent, General McClellan, and the morale of the Army of the Potomac.

Frustrated by the course of the war in the east, President Abraham Lincoln constantly found McClellan to be untrustworthy and openly defiant of the administration. That July, Lincoln sought to change the scope and goals of the war by issuing a proclamation freeing enslaved people in the Southern states. He felt he first needed a military victory to issue the proclamation, though. (loc)

Lee Moves North
CHAPTER ONE

This route follows portions of the Army of Northern Virginia from Manassas, Virginia, to Frederick, Maryland. The route includes infantry and cavalry movements and will highlight notable locations along the Confederate march into Maryland. The entire route is approximately 75 miles. For those wishing to follow the Federal advance into Maryland, use Chapter 2.

September 1862 saw the conclusion of a very active summer for General Lee and the Army of Northern Virginia. Lee successfully had cleared Virginia of two Federal armies, but the total victory he sought eluded him. Lee knew that just defeating the enemy in a battle was not enough—he needed to destroy the Federal army in a final battle. His plans to destroy Pope at the battle of Second Manassas were nearly realized, but Pope had held off Maj. Gen. James Longstreet's late afternoon assault and escaped to Fairfax Courthouse. Then Lee again tried to interpose himself between Washington, DC, and Pope's army at the battle of Ox Hill. Dogged by a slow march and poor performance at Ox Hill, the Army of Northern Virginia was plainly worn out. But as Lee noted about the Federal forces in his letter to Davis, "I did not think it would be advantageous to follow him farther. I had no

Sugarloaf Mountain looms over the Frederick County countryside. (kp)

Tour Stops

1. Manassas NB VC
2. Chantilly Battlefield
3. Dranesville Tavern
4. Harrison Hall
5. Mile Hill
6. White's Ford Park
7. McKimmey's Landing
8. Monocacy Aqueduct
9. Sugarloaf Mountain
10. Comus Inn
11. Monocacy River Ford
12. Carrollton Manor
13. Michael's Mill
14. Landon House
15. Best Farm

Confederates Enter Maryland Driving Tour

0   miles   8

Hal Jespersen

CONFEDERATES ENTER MARYLAND DRIVING TOUR— On September 5, 1862, the Army of Northern Virginia began crossing the Potomac River en masse. Lee's plan was to concentrate in Frederick, await developments from the Federal forces, and then possibly continue to move northwest. The part of Maryland the Confederates maneuvered in was mostly pro-Union in its sentiment, so Lee did not expect—or receive—an overly friendly welcome.

intention of attacking him in his fortifications, and am not prepared to invest them."

As he stated, Lee knew he could not attack the Federals behind the strong line of forts and entrenchments that encircled Washington. Lee, always seeking to hold the initiative, also knew that he could not remain inactive, as he continued to Davis, "still we cannot afford to be idle, and though weaker than our opponents in men and military equipment, must endeavor to harass if we cannot destroy them."

So, what should Lee do? Remaining in Northern Virginia was not practicable, a region devoid of supplies and devastated by Federal occupation. Also, as Joe Johnston had found out earlier in 1862, the region was nearly impossible to defend with the Federals controlling the Potomac River. Audacious in character, Lee disliked the idea of returning to central Virginia. Plus, giving up hard-fought ground could hurt the morale of his men. Lastly, by doing so, he would gain nothing strategically. The only alternative in Lee's mind called for another turning movement northward around the Federal army. This would be his third such movement since leaving Richmond. The first occurred along the Rappahannock River on August 24 by Maj. Gen. Thomas "Stonewall" Jackson's wing, then again on September 1 as Jackson marched to gain the flank or rear of Pope's army. Now, Lee proposed a different turning movement, one he knew could have long-lasting political and military impacts on the outcome of the war.

The "Confederates Enter Maryland" tour begins at the Manassas National Battlefield Park. The park interprets the First and Second Battles of Manassas (or Bull Run), The latter battle is often considered the starting point of the Maryland Campaign.

GPS: N 38.812965, W 77.521541

The battle of Second Manassas (or Bull Run) was one of Robert E. Lee's most complete victories. Pope hoped to destroy Jackson's wing of the Confederate army before Lee and Longstreet arrived. Pope argued throughout his life that McClellan's delay in arriving in northern Virginia with his Army of the Potomac led his own army to disaster. (loc)

TOUR STOP 1: MANASSAS NATIONAL BATTLEFIELD

The Second Battle of Manassas, fought August 28-30, 1862, was one of Confederate Gen. Robert E. Lee's most complete victories. Lee, in early August, split his army in half to deal with a new Federal threat, the Army of Virginia under Maj. Gen. John Pope. Lee made a strategic and bold move by ignoring the Army of the Potomac at Harrison's Landing east of Richmond and striking northward to take on Pope. After a series of Confederate flanking maneuvers, the two armies clashed on the old Manassas battlefield. The Confederates successfully held off Pope's attacks over the three days and completed a sweeping flank attack on the 30th. Federal casualties were nearly 14,000, and Confederate casualties were approximately 8,000. Regardless of the Confederate victory, Lee failed in his objective to destroy the Army of Virginia. Pope escaped toward Centreville on the night of August 30. On the following day, Lee ordered another flanking march to get into the retreating Federal army's rear at Fairfax Courthouse. This was Lee's last attempt to destroy Pope's army before it could return to the safety of the Washington, DC, fortifications.

Turn right out of the Visitor Center parking lot onto Route 234 (Sudley Road). At the next stop light, make a right onto Route 29 (Lee Highway). In approximately 1.3 miles you will cross Bull Run at Stone Bridge; here, on August 31, Confederate Gen. Robert E. Lee's horse reared up, throwing Lee to the ground, injuring both his hands. The parking lot for Stone Bridge will be on the left. Continue for 8.2 miles and take Route 608 (West Ox Road). This will be a right exit ramp, then a left turn onto West Ox Road. Travel 1.5 miles on West Ox Road and make a U-turn at the intersection with Monument Drive. The Ox Hill Battlefield Park will be on the right after the U-turn.

Today, a small Fairfax County park is all that is left of the battlefield. Many point to this park as the birthplace of the modern-day battlefield preservation movement. (ro)

GPS: N 38.864415, W 77.369809

TOUR STOP 2: OX HILL (CHANTILLY) BATTLEFIELD

On August 31, after his decisive victory at Second Manassas, Robert E. Lee ordered Stonewall Jackson's wing of the Army of Northern Virginia to turn the position of Pope's army at Centreville. Jackson marched via Sudley Springs, Gum Spring, and eastward along the Little River Turnpike (modern day Route 50). His objective was to force Pope from his strong Centreville position, gain the rear of the Federal army, and cut Pope's line of retreat near Fairfax Courthouse (modern day city of Fairfax). Jackson's exhausted columns moved slowly in rain and mud.

Meanwhile, Pope had lost all confidence in himself and his men. In his stressed mental state, he waffled between holding Centreville, fighting to the last, and withdrawing to the Washington defenses. On August 31, Pope received reports of Confederate cavalry in his rear at Chantilly, and later that night, near Jermantown. There, General James Ewell Brown "Jeb" Stuart's cavalry scouted in advance of Jackson along the Little River Turnpike. About sunset, Stuart observed Federal wagons moving eastward on the converging Warrenton Turnpike (Route 29). He quickly deployed his horse artillery and

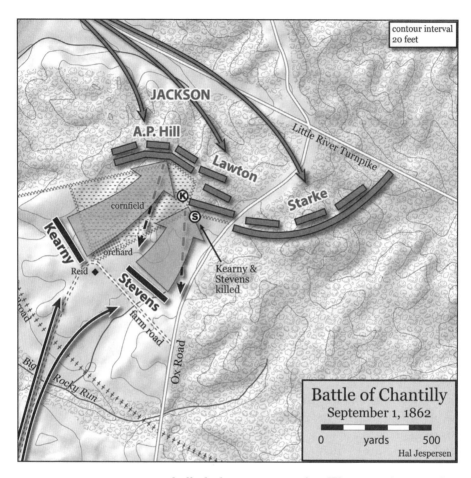

Battle of Chantilly
September 1, 1862

0   yards   500

Hal Jespersen

BATTLE OF CHANTILLY— On September 1, 1862, Confederate forces under Maj. Gen. Thomas "Stonewall" Jackson attempted another flank march to gain the rear of Maj. Gen. John Pope's Army of Virginia. Battle-worn and tired, the Confederates ran into Pope's column near Ox Hill along the Little River Turnpike. Fought during a severe thunderstorm, the fight was bloody but inconclusive.

shelled the wagon train. Those actions and a Federal reconnaissance the next morning alerted Pope to his precarious position. Pope sent troops eastward to Jermantown to block Jackson and protect his line of retreat. On the afternoon of September 1, Pope ordered the small IX Corps northward across country to the Little River Turnpike to block Jackson, west of Jermantown. When the IX Corps, supported by one division of III Corps, approached the turnpike, Jackson was already there.

The two forces clashed in the fields near Ox Hill. Fighting in a severe thunderstorm, the Federal attacks forced the numerically superior Confederates to deploy the majority of their troops to fend off the assaults. The short, bloody battle took the lives of Union generals Isaac Stevens and Philip Kearny. Casualties included more than 1,000 Federal troops and 516 Confederates in this affair. Monuments to Stevens and Kearny were erected in 1915. Today this small park is all that is left of the historic Ox Hill/Chantilly battlefield. Desperate efforts in 1986 to protect the monuments and preserve this park gave birth to the modern Civil War battlefield preservation movement.

Turn right out of the parking lot onto West Ox Road southward. Make a U-turn at the next possible intersection and take West Ox Road northward. Travel approximately 3.5 miles and take the left to stay on West Ox Road. After 1.1 miles, take a right onto Route 286 north (Fairfax County Parkway). Travel north for approximately 6.8 miles and take Route 7 west (Leesburg Pike). Once on Route 7, travel 0.2 miles, then turn right onto Dranesville Manor Drive. Immediately turn right into the Dranesville Tavern entrance road. The Civil War Trails marker is located in the parking lot.

GPS: N 39.008291, W 77.360635

STOP 3: DRANESVILLE TAVERN

After the battle of Ox Hill, Lee sent his cavalry under Stuart to scout ways around the Federals located in Fairfax Courthouse. Riding to the area of Flint Hill, Stuart concluded that the Federals were comfortably safe among the fortifications around Washington. Lee moved his infantry northwest along several roads to Dranesville. Lee's mind already tackled the "next step," and he formulated his plans in writing to his commander in chief. Writing Jefferson Davis on September 3, Lee stressed the benefits of crossing the Potomac River while also explaining the needs of his army (ammunition, clothing, and, most of all, shoes).

Fort C. F. Smith in Arlington County was one of dozens of forts built around Washington, DC, to protect the Federal capital. Lee knew that once the Federal army was behind the forts, he would have to look for other options to gain an advantage. (loc)

The only remaining building of the village of Dranesville, the Dranesville Tavern was moved a short distance when Route 7 was expanded to four lanes. Here on September 3, the Army of Northern Virginia was camped in and around the village. Maj. Gen. Jeb Stuart used the tavern as his headquarters. (kp)

Lee believed his army's operations in Northern territory ensured Richmond's safety because the Federal armies would focus on him. Lee was often overheard saying, "Richmond was never so safe as when her defenders were absent." Before receiving a response from Davis, Lee began to move his men westward along the Leesburg Turnpike on September 4. Before his infantry moved, he ordered the 2nd Virginia Cavalry to Leesburg to clear the area of the Northern partisan "Loudoun Rangers."

Lee's plan called for the army to march to Leesburg and to cross into Maryland, using the various fords along the Potomac in northern Loudoun County, Virginia. Lee also expected reinforcements from central Virginia, including divisions under Maj. Gens. D. H. Hill, Lafayette McLaws and and Brig. Gen. John Walker.

As Lee planned his movement, he believed Pope still would command the Federal army, then situated around Washington. Lee was yet to find out that Maj. Gen. George B. McClellan now led the Federal forces in and around

Washington. As the Confederates marched westward, a disagreement between Maj. Gen. A. P. Hill and Stonewall Jackson developed over Hill's handling of his division during the march. Soon, Jackson put Hill under arrest, and Hill marched at the rear of his division.

The ca. 1850 tavern building (moved 130 feet from its original location due to the widening of Route 7) and the Bloomfield house across Route 7 are the remains of Dranesville village. Local tradition claims the yard around Bloomfield served as the location of Stonewall Jackson's headquarters while Jeb Stuart established his headquarters at Dranesville Tavern.

Across the street from the Dranesville Tavern sits Bloomfield. Built in about 1850, the house was the home of the Carper family. Local tradition has it that the family offered the home to "Stonewall" Jackson for his headquarters when he arrived here in September 1862. He supposedly refused and set up his headquarters tent in the yard. Nearby was also the headquarters of Robert E. Lee, and from here he sent his message to Jefferson Davis about his plans to enter Maryland. (kp)

⟶ TO STOP 4

Return to Route 7 (Leesburg Pike), then take a left to head west. Travel west for 13.4 miles (this will take you into Leesburg on Route 7 Business). Once in downtown Leesburg, make a right onto King Street north. In about 0.2 miles, a Civil War Trails marker stands on the left side of the street in front of Harrison Hall. Street parking is allowed. Please be cautious crossing the street.

GPS: N 39.117729, W 77.563572

STOP 4: HARRISON HALL

Construction started in 1780 and, by 1860, the building was completed for Henry and Jane Harrison. During the nearby battle of Ball's Bluff (October 21, 1861), the house served as a Confederate hospital. The town of Leesburg and the Harrisons welcomed Lee here on September 4. The town's citizens gave the marching Confederates a very warm welcome. Soon, Lee sought medical care for his arms and hands from Dr. Samuel Jackson, whose home still stands to the right of Harrison Hall.

Lee also took time to visit with his son, Robert Lee, Jr., and local leader John Janney. Janney, though opposed to secession, had served as President of the Virginia Secession

Founded in 1758 in honor of Thomas Lee and the Lee family, Leesburg was at the intersection of the Carolina Road (Route 15) and the road that led from Alexandria to the Shenandoah Valley (Route 7). In 1862, it served as an important crossroads as the Confederates could either continue west to the Shenandoah Valley, or turn north and cross the Potomac into Maryland. (lm)

One of the larger homes in town in 1862, Harrison Hall offered a welcome reprieve for Lee and his staff. Next door still sits the home of doctor Samuel Jackson who worked on Lee's injured arms. Of all the events that took place here in September 1862, the most important to Lee was probably seeing his son, Robert Lee, Jr., on a short visit. (kp)

Convention and had officially given Lee command of Virginia's forces in 1861. Janney's home still stands at 10 Cornwall Street, still a private residence.

On September 5, Lee held a meeting with some of his top generals to determine the army's strategy as it moved into Maryland. Lee announced to his lieutenants his plans to enter Maryland and then, if events allowed, the Cumberland Valley of Pennsylvania. The day before, Lee had already ordered the division under D. H. Hill to enter Maryland, using three fords in northern Loudoun County. The army would retain its confusing command structure of divisions and wing commanders (Jackson and Longstreet), with some divisions reporting directly to Lee. At this point, Lee knew the Federal garrisons held Harpers Ferry and Martinsburg. He believed as the Confederates moved northward these Federals would abandon their posts, thus allowing Lee to change his communication and supply route to pass through the Shenandoah Valley, rather than northern Virginia. The basis of Lee's plan depended on a slow Federal response. He underestimated the condition of the Federal army, as he would soon find out.

Lee coordinated his army's crossing of the Potomac and entrance into Maryland. He also gave strict orders to do everything possible to reduce straggling and to respect private property of Maryland citizens. It is questionable how much support Lee believed he would get from the citizens of western Maryland, but most historians agree Lee had no delusions that thousands of Marylanders would join the Confederate army. He sent President Davis another dispatch and then began the move into Maryland.

Continue north on King Street; in 1.5 miles continue north on Route 15. In 0.3 miles make a left onto Tutt Lane. Once on Tutt Lane, the Civil War Trails marker will be on the first left.

GPS: N 39.143235, W 77.550163

STOP 5: MILE HILL

Though the majority of Loudoun County voted for secession in 1861, a large portion of the population still was pro-Union. Also, geographically, the county is surrounded on two sides by the Potomac River and Maryland. This allowed for Federal-based cavalry units and partisans to operate in the area; Loudoun native Samuel Means led one such force: the Loudoun Rangers. These Rangers and men from Cole's Maryland Cavalry were reportedly harassing pro-Confederate citizens in Leesburg, so on September 1, Lee ordered Col. Thomas Munford and his 2nd Virginia Cavalry to clear out the Federal partisans.

Arriving near Leesburg on September 2, Munford pushed the Federals through town to here on Mile Hill. Munford devised a plan to lure the Federals to attack him while he sent a portion of his regiment to the northeast to get behind the Federals. The plan worked, and once Cole ordered a charge on Munford's men near

John Janney was a well-respected political leader in Leesburg. Janney served as the president of the Virginia Secession Convention and worked hard for moderation. As a Quaker, he objected originally to secession and the military preparation for war but voted with the majority once secession was a foregone conclusion. As president of the secession convention, he offered Robert E. Lee command of the Virginia forces. While Lee was in Leesburg, he paid a visit to Janney, who lived a few blocks from Harrison Hall. (lva)

Col. Thomas Munford was being groomed for promotion in the Maryland Campaign, given temporary command of Beverly Robertson's cavalry brigade. A VMI graduate, Munford was a capable officer but did not live up to the high expectations some placed on him. (phcw)

Before the war, Samuel Means ran the largest mill in Loudoun County and had business interests in neighboring Maryland. He was a staunch Unionist and began to assist Federal cavalry patrols into Loudoun County. In 1862, he was given a commission of captain and authorized to raise a local unit of pro-Union cavalry known as the Loudoun Rangers. (lvar)

Leesburg, the other segment of his regiment attacked the Federals from the rear. The result was an absolute rout. Munford suffered two dead and six wounded while the Federals lost 11 killed, 20 wounded, and 47 captured (out of 160 men).

Return to Tutt Lane and take a right. Upon reaching Route 15, take a left and travel for 4.6 miles. Immediately to the left as you make this turn is a large spring called "Big Spring." Here, Confederates stopped to fill canteens, and many wrote about the spring in their letters. The Army of Northern Virginia used many of these fields as campsites before crossing into Maryland, to the east. Take a right onto Route 657 (Spinks Ferry Road), travel 1.5 miles, and make a right onto Route 661 (Limestone School Road). Travel 1 mile and make a left onto Route 656 (Hibler Road). After 1.1 miles, the entrance to White's Ford Park will be on the right. Follow the park road all the way to the end, where a path leads to the area of White's Ford.

GPS: N 39.187521, W 77.483244

STOP 6: WHITE'S FORD PARK

Lee was apprehensive about crossing the Potomac River east of the mountains. But when D. H. Hill's division crossed the Potomac on September 4 and met little resistance, Lee surmised the Federals were not in central Maryland in force. Lee planned on using the various fords in northern Loudoun to cross his men quickly. Here at White's Ford, Stonewall Jackson's wing began to cross on September 5. The first regiment was the 10th Virginia Infantry, and soon, bands struck up the popular tune "Maryland! My Maryland!" Many of the Confederates took off their shoes for the trip through the river. One soldier in the 49th Georgia wrote, "Never did I behold so many naked legs in my life."

The ford was not well known and required some work along the banks to allow wheeled vehicles, such as artillery, wagons, and ambulances, to cross. This took time, and the

Thousands of Confederates crossed the Potomac River fords near Leesburg. The crossing was well documented by many Confederates, who knew it was a momentous occasion. Only token Federal skirmishers waited on the Maryland side, and Confederates easily brushed them aside. Time was of the essence for Lee's army, so some men crossed at night. (loc)

crossing proceeded more slowly than Jackson liked. Confederate cavalry under General Stuart also crossed here, though this added to the traffic jam along the country roads. Stuart and Jackson were both across the Potomac by 6:00 p.m. on September 5.

Here, on the morning of September 6, Longstreet's infantry crossed the Potomac along with the army's commander, Robert E. Lee, in an ambulance because of his hand injuries. Other Confederate units under Brig. Gen. George B. Anderson and Brig. Gen. John Walker crossed just north at Cheek's Ford. Once the Confederate infantry crossed, their first mission would be to disrupt traffic on the C&O Canal as well as the B&O Railroad. Stuart's cavalry headed to Poolesville, Maryland, to screen the Confederate march and to look out for a possible Federal advance from Washington.

Exit the park and make a left onto Hibler Road. In 1.1 miles, make a right onto Route 661 (Limestone School Road). In 1 mile, make a left onto Route 657 (Spinks Ferry Road) and follow this to Route 15. Take

Brig. Gen. Roswell Ripley was born in Ohio but moved to South Carolina before the war. Ripley had extensive military experience, having served in Mexico and in the Seminole Wars. When South Carolina seceded, he cast his lot with his adoptive home of South Carolina. He commanded a mixed brigade of Georgia and North Carolina troops. He was severely wounded at the battle of Antietam. (phcw)

Today, the Northern Virginia Regional Park Authority preserves White's Ford. Visitors can use the kayak/canoe launch to access the Potomac River. The scene today is much quieter than it was on September 5-6, 1862. (kp)

At the beginning of the war, skirmishing between Federal and Confederate forces took place all along the Potomac River. At McKimmey's Landing in 1861, Stonewall Jackson ordered the bridge that led into Maryland burned. One of the first skirmishes here led to the first war death in Loudoun County. Private Cumberland George Orrison of the 6th Virginia Cavalry was mortally wounded when a Federal raiding party snuck across the river and attacked his detachment near the location of the burned bridge. (ro)

a right onto Route 15 (north) and travel 7 miles; there, make a left onto Route 672 (Lovettsville Road) then take your immediate right. A Civil War Trails marker on the right focuses on the events that took place here in 1861. The Potomac River can be accessed near the boat ramp.

GPS: N 39.271193, W 77.548999

STOP 7: McKimmey's Landing

Here, near the location of the current Potomac River bridge stood a toll bridge in 1861. This was one of the major crossings into Maryland from Virginia and the only bridge between Harpers Ferry and Washington, DC. In the spring of 1861, then Brig. Gen. Thomas Jackson ordered the bridge burned to keep Federals from using it to gain access into Loudoun County.

On September 4, 1862, Maj. Gen. D. H. Hill's division received orders to cross the Potomac and disrupt the C&O Canal and B&O Railroad. Hill was also Lee's way of testing for any Federal opposition in central Maryland. A successful crossing by Hill would determine if and where Lee crossed the rest of his army. D. H. Hill had five brigades in his division. He ordered Brig. Gen. George B. Anderson's brigade to the Virginia side of the Potomac opposite Berlin; there, he could harass railroad traffic with his artillery, allowing the brigades of Colquitt and Rodes to cross at Cheek's Ford while Garland's brigade crossed at Noland's Ferry. Here at McKimmey's Landing, the brigade under Brig. Gen. Roswell Ripley crossed around 3:00 p.m. Hill's men were the first Confederates of the Army of Northern Virginia into Maryland.

Turn left out of the driveway and turn left onto Route 15 north. Cross the Potomac River and make the first right onto Route 28 (Clay Street). Continue for 4.7 miles (through Point of Rocks), then make a right to stay on Route 28 (Dickerson Road). Continue for 3.4 miles and make a right onto Mouth of Monocacy

Road. Continue for 1.2 miles and bear left toward the parking lot of the Monocacy Aqueduct. A Civil War Trails marker stands along the trail to the aqueduct.

GPS: N 39.222562, W 77.450048

STOP 8: MONOCACY AQUEDUCT

Completed in 1833, the Monocacy Aqueduct was one of eleven aqueducts built along the C&O Canal. The aqueduct acted as a bridge for the canal to cross over rivers and streams in the canal's path. The Monocacy Aqueduct is one of the most impressive, still standing as a monument to American civil engineering.

On September 4-5, D. H. Hill's division worked in the area to destroy this segment of the canal. His men spent most of their time draining the channel by digging holes in the earthen berms along the canal. Destroying the aqueduct itself would require more time, engineering, and gun powder than Hill wanted to spend. Also, local canal employee Thomas Walter pleaded with the Confederates to leave the aqueduct alone. Local lore gives Walter the credit of saving the aqueduct, though, on the night of September 9, John Walker's division was ordered here to destroy the aqueduct on its way back to Virginia

The Monocacy Aqueduct was quite an engineering feat when it was built in 1832. The fact that the Confederates tried several times to destroy it and failed proves it was well built. It still survives today as a testament to 19th century engineering and masonry. (ro)

The Monocacy Aqueduct today is a popular stop on the Maryland Civil War Trails and with hikers and cyclists. (ro)

Brig. Gen, John George Walker had a quick stint in the Army of Northern Virginia. Promoted to command in January 1862, he led a division in the Maryland Campaign. He was then promoted and transferred to the Trans-Mississippi Department in November. Many historians have used Walker's postwar accounts of the Maryland Campaign; however, today, some of his interpretations have proven to be inaccurate. (phcw)

and Harpers Ferry. Walker's men failed on several attempts to destroy the aqueduct due to its engineering and their lack of tools and knowledge.

Soon after Walker's departure, Federals under Darius Couch arrived and protected the aqueduct from further Confederate attacks. The federal's presence forced Walker to cross the Potomac at Point of Rocks, not at nearby Cheek's Ford as he was ordered. Walker continued back into Virginia and played a crucial role in the capture of Harpers Ferry on September 15.

Return the way you came; upon reaching Route 28, continue straight on Mouth of Monocacy Road. In 0.4 miles, take a left onto Mt. Ephraim Road. Travel for 2.5 miles to the Sugarloaf Mountain parking lot. Take in the Civil War Trails marker on the left in the parking area. If you want to drive up Sugarloaf Mountain and see the location of the signal stations, continue through the gate on Sugarloaf Mountain Drive to the West View Parking Lot. Remember, follow all posted regulations. Sugarloaf Mountain is owned and operated by Stronghold Incorporated; donations are accepted.

GPS: N 39.251646, W 77.393378

STOP 9: SUGARLOAF MOUNTAIN

Sugarloaf Mountain is one of the highest points in central Maryland—its heights provide views east all the way to Washington, DC. Its geography made it a strategic location during the Civil War, and the Federals established a signal station atop Sugarloaf in 1861. When the Confederates moved into Maryland in early September, the Federals first spotted them from here at the signal station. As the Confederates moved northward, Confederate cavalry commander Jeb Stuart's mission was to screen the infantry. Stuart knew the importance of Sugarloaf and detailed cavalry to capture the mountain and station.

On September 5, the two Federals working the signal station realized they would be isolated and decided to head eastward. As they did so, they captured a Confederate courier who possessed dispatches from Confederate President Jefferson Davis to Lee. Luckily for the Confederates, the 1st North Carolina cavalry overtook the trio, so the courier continued his ride to Lee.

With the capture of Sugarloaf, the Confederates now had a strategic vantage point to keep an eye on the Army of the Potomac. The capture also isolated the garrison at Harpers Ferry for a time as their telegraph and signal communications to the east were cut. Soon lead elements of the Army of the Potomac arrived in the form of Federal cavalry, and a running cavalry battle was fought in the fields around Sugarloaf Mountain.

Brig. Gen. Darius Couch was a favorite of George McClellan's—so much so that when he tried to resign due to failing health after Seven Days' Campaign, McClellan failed to act on it. Couch stayed on, but his health would continue to affect him in the Maryland Campaign. (loc)

From the parking area at the base of Sugarloaf Mountain, take Comus Road east and travel 2.4 miles. Take a left onto Route 109 (Old Hundred Road) and then the next left into the parking lot for the Comus Inn. The Civil War Trails markers will be in the parking lot to the right of Comus Inn.

GPS: N 39.248195, W 77.349976

Today, one can drive to the crest of Sugarloaf Mountain and visit the site of the signal station that was captured here on September 5. This view west is very similar to the view of 1862. (ro)

A Republican Congressman from Illinois before the war, John Farnsworth used his political clout to form his own regiment of cavalry, the 8th Illinois. He served in the Peninsula and Maryland campaigns but then resigned in 1863 to return to Congress. He was also able to use his political position to secure a lieutenant's commission for his 24-year-old nephew, Elon John Farnsworth of Gettysburg fame. (loc)

STOP 10: COMUS INN

As Confederate infantry moved northward to consolidate in Frederick, Lee ordered Stuart and his cavalry to screen the army's movement and provide intelligence on the whereabouts of the Army of the Potomac. Lee believed the Federal morale was severely damaged by the defeat at Second Manassas, and he thought it would take time for McClellan to organize and build up the strength of his army. Lee soon found out that he underestimated the Federals.

The cavalry fighting that took place here at Mt. Ephraim Crossroads on September 10 was the latest in a days-long series of running fights that had started at Poolesville on September 8. Here, several hundred Virginia cavalrymen under Col. Thomas Munford fought a back-and-forth battle with the 6th US Cavalry. The Regulars' efforts failed to capture the crossroads and the mountaintop looming above it. Munford's stand here forced Union cavalry commander Alfred Pleasonton to call for help. Finally, on September 11, thanks to a combined Federal cavalry and infantry effort, Munford's dogged men gave up their defense of Sugarloaf Mountain and fell back toward Frederick. By 3:00 p.m., on September 11, the Army of the Potomac occupied the coveted mountain.

Using the terrain to their advantage, the Confederates held off the Federal cavalry and artillery (placed on the hills in front of you). Both sides fought to a standstill on September 10, and the next day the Confederate cavalry was ordered to pull back toward Frederick. At that time, Lee ordered his infantry columns westward to the passes of South Mountain. Soon, the Federal cavalry would be in close pursuit of the Army of Northern Virginia.

Make a right onto Route 109 (Old Hundred Road), travel for 2.4 miles to Barnesville, and make a right onto Barnesville Road. Travel for 2.2 miles before making a left onto Mt. Ephraim Road. Travel 0.5 miles and make a right onto Mouth of Monocacy Road, then take your first right onto Route 28 (Dickerson Road). Travel for 4.7 miles and make a right into the garden center. The Civil War Trails marker is at the garden center entrance.

GPS: N 39.280035, W 77.463507

STOP 11: CARROLLTON MANOR

Most of the Confederate infantry that crossed the fords of the Potomac from Loudoun County into Maryland marched on this road to Frederick. The Buckeystown Pike, a major road in central Maryland, intersected many prosperous farms. Lee planned to consolidate his infantry in Frederick, rest his men, then move northwest to possibly invade Pennsylvania. From Frederick, Lee could threaten Washington, Baltimore, and Harrisburg. Lee also hoped the rich farms of the area could supply his men with much needed supplies. He ordered his men not to forage without paying for the items taken, albeit typically in depreciated Confederate money.

As early as September 5, this road and the farms around it witnessed thousands of marching

Today a popular historic restaurant and event rental venue, the Comus Inn was once the home of Robert Johnson. The house in 1862 was much different from what it is today. Originally a small log home, the house was enlarged several times to its modern-day appearance. The original log section of the home is on the northern end of the structure. (kp)

Confederates and camp sites. Numerous Confederates picked green corn, which when eaten gave many severe stomach issues. The first Confederates to move through the area were under Stonewall Jackson and D. H. Hill. Many of the men were threadbare, barefoot, and hungry. One Northern news correspondent wrote, "the troops are all in a most filthy condition." Another local resident wrote, "the scratching they kept up gave warrant of vermin in abundance." Many could not believe this was the vaunted Army of Northern Virginia that had handed defeat after defeat to their Union armies.

On September 6, Jackson decided to mount a new horse given to him by a local resident. As Jackson spurred the animal, it reared and fell backwards, leaving Jackson badly bruised on the ground. He rested for thirty minutes, then travelled in an ambulance in his troop column headed for Frederick. Jackson recovered quickly enough, however, to ride his horse along the campaign route. The Confederates headed toward Monocacy Junction and then entered Frederick from the east.

Thousands of Confederates from Stonewall Jackson's command camped in these fields near Carrolton Manor. Many of these fields provided green corn to the soldiers—many of whom would remember the corn from the sickness it caused. The rolling farm landscape has changed little in 150 years. (kp)

Make a right onto Route 28 (Buckeystown Road) and travel for 4 miles into Buckeystown. Make a right onto Route 880 (Michaels Mill Road) and travel 1.1 miles. Make a left into the parking lot for the Buckeystown Community Park. The Civil War Trails maker is located on the far end of the parking lot.

GPS: N 39.327284, W 77.416002

Though only 800 feet high, Sugarloaf Mountain is more noticeable because it is not part of a nearby mountain chain. It is referred to as a monadnock, an isolated mountain rising abruptly from level surrounding land. The mountain played a significant role in the Civil War as a lookout/signal station in several campaigns. (kp)

STOP 12: MICHAEL'S MILL/BUCKEYSTOWN

A stone bridge near here took the Urbanna Road across the Monocacy River. One of the few bridges in the area, this crossing was important for the Confederate army as it moved north to Frederick. On September 6, 1862, Confederates encamped here on both sides of the river and commented on the amount of flour being stored in the nearby Delaplaine Mill (now Michael's Mill). With the B&O Railroad cut by the Confederates, the miller was forced to store the grain instead of shipping it via railroad eastward. The mill was owned by the Grove family, which opened up the mill and warehouse to marching Confederates. Local legend has it that the family's slaves cooked short cakes for the hungry soldiers.

Take a left out of the parking lot and make a left onto Route 80 (Fingerboard Road). Continue on Route 80 for 4.2 miles. Make a left onto Urbana Pike. The Landon House is at the corner; use the pull-off on the right from Urbana Pike.

GPS: N 39.326159, W 77.348636

The Delaplaine Mill, known today as Michael's Mill, was one of the oldest gristmills in Frederick County. The first mill was built on the site ca. 1739. Increased in size, the large mill was in operation until the 1950s. It was in this mill during the Maryland Campaign that Confederate soldiers sought a thousand barrels of flour. (kp)

Legend has it that this building was built in 1754 in Virginia and moved here in 1846. The building has served as home, female seminary, and military school. In 1862, it was known as the Landon Female Academy and served as a school for girls. It was here on September 8 that Jeb Stuart held his famous "Sabers and Roses Ball." The building also served as a hospital and, today, is surrounded by a fast-growing community. (kp)

Stop 13: Landon House

In 1862, the Landon House served as the Landon Female Academy. The building, originally built in Virginia in 1754, was deconstructed and moved here in 1846. Stuart placed portions of his cavalry in a wide arc east of Frederick, covering approaches from Poolesville, Rockville, and Baltimore. He then set up his headquarters, here at Urbana, as a control center for his cavalry.

On the night of September 8, Stuart's staff officer Maj. Heros von Borcke decided to host a grand ball for local ladies and the Confederate cavalry. Many of the Confederates were dressed in their best uniforms and enjoyed the gaiety of the occasion. The 18th Mississippi band serenaded the party-goers, and plenty of food and drink were available. Around midnight a courier arrived and reported an attack on Hampton's cavalry at their outpost near Hyattstown. Most of the men saddled up to confront the Federal cavalry. It turned out to be a small affair and the Confederates repulsed the Federal cavalry.

Soon, the men returned here to celebrate their "victory."

The Federal cavalry probes at Hyattstown and Barnesville proved that the Federals were not dealing cautiously with the Confederate invasion of Maryland.

Return to Urbana Pike and take the first right onto Sugarloaf Parkway. At the traffic circle, take the third exit, Route 355 (Worthington Boulevard). Stay on Route 355 (becomes Urbana Pike) for 4.1 miles. The entrance to the Best Farm Stop at Monocacy National Battlefield will be on your left. Take the gravel road to the parking area where there will be interpretive markers explaining the events here in 1862 (Maryland Campaign) and 1864 (battle of Monocacy).

GPS: N 39.370532, W 77.398792

One of the most noticeable foreign nationals in the Confederate army, Maj. Heros von Borcke served on Stuart's staff. At 6' 4" and 240 pounds, he was much larger than a typical cavalryman. Originally from Prussia, where he served in the military, Borcke came to America to fight in the Southern army and flee his creditors back home. Borcke was severely wounded in June 1863 and returned to Prussia in 1865. His memoirs of his service in the Civil War are still popular today. (phcw)

STOP 14: BEST FARM/MONOCACY NATIONAL BATTLEFIELD

Near here at Best Grove, Confederate Gens. Stonewall Jackson, James Longstreet, D. H. Hill, and Robert E. Lee established their headquarters from September 6 – 10. Best Grove, described as a grove of large oaks two miles east of Frederick, was owned by the Trail family, but the Best family rented the farm in 1862. The Best farm also became the home to thousands of Confederate infantry on the march.

As Lee settled in, he began to consider what to do next. Surely his move to Frederick was known in Washington by now. Stuart's cavalry actively fought off Federal cavalry thrusts from the east. On September 8, Lee issued a proclamation to the people of Maryland, promising that the Confederates were not looking to enforce their will on the civilians. "We know no enemies among you," the proclamation stated, and it welcomed all who chose to freely join their fellow Southerners.

Lee also issued general orders to his army, restating that a lack of discipline would not be tolerated, and he announced the victory of

Confederate Gen. Kirby Smith at Richmond, Kentucky. Now, the army knew they participated in a concerted Southern effort to move the front of the war into the Northern states, not just a lone thrust into Maryland.

While at Best Grove, Lee learned Confederate President Jefferson Davis was on his way north with former Maryland governor, Enoch Lowe. Lee had requested Lowe join him in Maryland, possibly as an advisor and possible rallying figure for pro-Confederate citizens. Lee, though, politely told Davis to stay in Virginia since he was too important to risk on the front line. Lee most surely preferred to operate without political interference.

Today, the location of the Best Farm is a rural oasis in the rapidly growing city of Frederick, Maryland, as part of the Monocacy National Battlefield Park. Many theories suggest that the Best Farm is the location where Federals discovered Lee's "Lost Orders" while more modern theories place the location closer to Frederick. (cm)

On September 9, Lee wrote one of the more famous orders of the Civil War. From his headquarters, he issued Special Orders No. 191, laying out the lines of march and goals for each division. By now, Lee also knew that the Federal garrisons in Martinsburg and Harpers Ferry had not left their posts. He therefore ordered Jackson, McLaws, and Walker to concentrate on

the garrisons and to force either their surrender or their withdrawal. Lee needed to reestablish his line of supply and communications through the Shenandoah Valley, but these two Federal garrisons impeded this objective. The orders also designated Hagerstown as the point where the divergent Confederate forces would concentrate after Martinsburg and Harpers Ferry were captured. It was a bold and risky move as Lee divided his already outnumbered force in a far and wide fashion. The Federals under McClellan at that point were only a day or two march away from Frederick. The move's success also depended upon Lee's expectation that Harpers Ferry and Martinsburg would be secured by September 12, just three days later— an unreasonable expectation. Even worse, a lost copy of Special Orders No. 191 fell into George B. McClellan's possession on September 13 (see Chapter 2, Stop 13).

The outcome of Lee's campaign into Maryland hung in the balance during the crucial next phase of the operation.

A native of Loudoun County, Lt. Col. Robert Chilton was on familiar ground in September 1862. Chilton served on Lee's small staff and rose to the position of chief. Chilton is best known for his part in the many stories surrounding Special Orders 191, the "Lost Orders." (phcw)

McClellan Responds
CHAPTER TWO

This route follows portions of the Federal Army of Virginia and the Army of the Potomac from Manassas, Virginia, to Frederick, Maryland. The route includes infantry and cavalry movements and will highlight notable locations along the Federal march into Maryland. The entire route is approximately 90 miles. For those wishing to follow the Confederate advance into Maryland, use Chapter 1.

The year 1862 began promisingly for the Northern war effort. Federals crowned western battlefields with victory, and George B. McClellan's waterborne campaign against Richmond started with great potential. The War Department even closed recruiting offices, anticipating a quick win.

By early summer, McClellan's offensive in the East stalled after a severe setback during the Seven Days' Battles in late June and early July forced his army away from the Confederate capital. Federal successes in the West dwindled, also. A new Federal army under John Pope coalesced on June 26, 1862, planning to take the overland route and threaten Richmond from the north. Meanwhile, officials in Washington ordered McClellan's Army of the Potomac off the Peninsula. Once Pope's and McClellan's forces united between Richmond

Sugarloaf Mountain's height above the surrounding landscape made it a key piece of terrain for both armies during the Maryland Campaign. (kp)

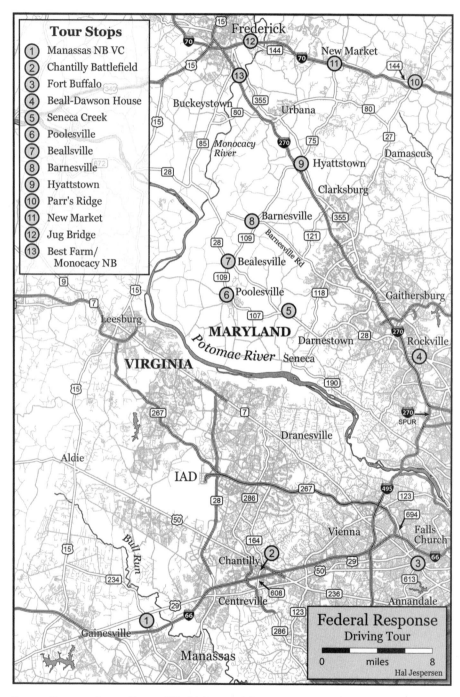

Tour Stops

1. Manassas NB VC
2. Chantilly Battlefield
3. Fort Buffalo
4. Beall-Dawson House
5. Seneca Creek
6. Poolesville
7. Beallsville
8. Barnesville
9. Hyattstown
10. Parr's Ridge
11. New Market
12. Jug Bridge
13. Best Farm/ Monocacy NB

Federal Response Driving Tour

0   miles   8

Hal Jespersen

FEDERAL RESPONSE DRIVING TOUR— This driving tour follows the routes of the Army of the Potomac's three wings as they marched from Washington, DC, to Frederick, Maryland. Many cavalry fights erupted during the early stages of the campaign as George McClellan sought to learn Lee's intentions and positions.

and Washington City, this overwhelmingly large army could march down on the defenders of the Confederate capital.

Before the two Federal hosts joined, Pope's army encountered Robert E. Lee's Confederate Army of Northern Virginia in early August. The two forces clashed at Cedar Mountain on August 9, triggering a campaign of maneuver and small battles. Stonewall Jackson, at the van of Lee's army, began a march on August 25 to break the stalemate and strike Pope's supply line at Manassas Junction, forcing the Federals back toward their capital. Pope blindly sought out Jackson's command, proclaiming to "bag the whole crowd."

While the Army of Virginia moved to concentrate, Jackson's forces revealed themselves, ensconced behind an unfinished railroad cut, not far from the old Bull Run battlefield. A sharp firefight broke out between the two sides on the evening of August 28. The cat and mouse game had ended.

Begin the "Federals Respond" chapter tour at the Manassas National Battlefield Visitor Center, 6511 Sudley Road, Manassas, Virginia 20109.

GPS: N 38.812965, W 77.521541

STOP 1: MANASSAS NATIONAL BATTLEFIELD

John Pope remained confident, on the morning of August 29, that he had found an isolated Stonewall Jackson and enacted plans to ensure his enemy's destruction. Diversionary attacks along his line would keep Jackson's eyes away from Pope's main effort—a strike against Jackson's right nearly two miles to the west. Several attacks went forward against the Confederate position, each hoping to be the anvil to Pope's hammer blow. Some of the assaults broke through, but Pope's

Stonewall Jackson's successful flank march around John Pope's Army of Virginia netted his soldiers many spoils when they sacked the Federal supply depot at Manassas Junction on August 27, 1862. (b&l)

For the second time in thirteen months, a Federal army retreated across the Stone Bridge spanning Bull Run following defeat on the battlefield. (b&l)

main effort never happened—the rest of Robert E. Lee's arriving army blocked its attack path.

The Federal commander remained ignorant of the newly arrived enemy forces and the next day threw forward more attacks against Jackson's steadfast men. They nearly broke, but in the end, repulsed Pope's attacks.

Suddenly, 25,000 Confederates—the rest of Lee's army—unleashed themselves on the weakened left flank of the Federal forces, sweeping it back to Henry Hill. Pope and his subordinate officers worked to establish the last line of defense here to save his army and preserve its escape route back to Washington.

Ultimately, the United States forces met the same fate here that they had thirteen months earlier in July 1861. Pope pulled his men back to Centreville across Bull Run to the east while he plotted the next course of action. His army did not hurry in a panic back to its new lines, but it left behind about 14,000 of its soldiers on the fields of Manassas, compared to approximately 8,000 enemy casualties.

Turn right out of the Visitor Center parking lot onto Route 234 (Sudley Road). At the next stoplight, make a right onto Route 29 (Lee Highway). In about 1.3 miles, cross Bull Run at Stone Bridge. It was here that Confederate Gen. Robert E. Lee was injured on August 31 when his horse reared up and threw Lee to the ground, injuring both his hands. The parking lot for Stone Bridge will be on the left. Continue for 8.2 miles and take Route 608 (West Ox Road). This will be a right exit ramp, then a left turn onto West Ox Road. Travel 1.5 miles on West Ox Road and make a U-turn at the intersection with Monument Drive. The Ox Hill Battlefield Park will be on the right after the U-turn.

GPS: N 38.864415, W 77.369809

STOP 2: OX HILL BATTLEFIELD PARK

By September 1, John Pope realized the wisdom in pulling his army back even closer to Washington. The Confederates, meanwhile, attempted to prevent the Army of Virginia from escaping and began another march to interpose themselves between the Federals and Washington. Pope wrote that "this movement . . . will force me to attack his advance," and he dispatched Brig. Gen. Isaac Stevens's IX Corps to do just that while Pope put more of his soldiers into a blocking defensive position at Jermantown to the east.

Stevens hurled his troops at Jackson's defensive line, posted behind a rail fence bordering a cornfield south of the Little River Turnpike. Initially, the blue-clad soldiers pierced the enemy's line. Isaac Stevens himself stepped into the breakthrough, but a Confederate bullet to the head instantly knocked him out of the fight. His death, coupled with "one of the wildest rainstorms I ever witnessed," recalled one participant, stalled the IX Corps's attack.

One-armed Phil Kearny's III Corps division arrived at Stevens's left as support, pressing forward through the stalks of corn. Kearny, like

Isaac Stevens graduated first in his 1839 West Point class and served as the territorial governor of Washington before the Civil War. (loc)

Phil Kearny lost his left arm from a wound received in the Mexican War at Churubusco. That did not stop him from becoming a hard-hitting division commander in the Army of the Potomac until his death at Chantilly. (loc)

Stevens, led from the front. Confusion from battle smoke, the driving rain, booming thunder, and the fading daylight took hold on the battlefield as Kearny rode forward to locate the Rebels. An enemy bullet felled him, too, and Kearny died before he hit the ground.

Darkness finally ended the inconclusive fight. Pope's defense at Jermantown blunted the latest Confederate threat. Fearing a worse situation when the sun rose, however, he ordered his army back to Washington's fortifications that night.

Turn right out of the battlefield parking lot onto West Ox Road and make a U-turn at the next possible intersection. Travel north on West Ox Road and in 0.2 miles take the ramp onto US Route 50 East. Go 2.5 miles and turn left onto US Route 29 North/US Route 50 East/Fairfax Boulevard/Arlington Boulevard. Travel 6.5 miles before turning right onto Sleepy Hollow Road, Route 613. Turn left in 0.2 miles into the parking lot of the Seven Corners Fire Station. The sign for Fort Buffalo is adjacent to the parking lot.

GPS: N 38.870512, W 77.156959

The October 2, 1915, dedication of the Stevens and Kearny monuments on the Chantilly battlefield included both Union and Confederate veterans in attendance, including Isaac Stevens's son, Hazard. (kp)

STOP 3: FORT BUFFALO

"Unless something can be done to restore tone to this army it will melt away before you know it," the downtrodden John Pope told Henry Halleck on the morning of September 2.

John Pope arrived in this vicinity later that day, "covered with dust," appearing "worn and serious." The recently re-appointed commander of the forces in Washington, George McClellan, met him "and they exchanged greetings." McClellan then told Pope where to place his command before dismissing him.

Suddenly, word spread down the line that George McClellan was once again in command. Men cheered the news and yelled "with wild delight." Now, George McClellan's task called for reorganizing portions of several large forces into one army able to keep the Confederates out of the capital and, possibly, to repulse an enemy incursion across the Potomac River.

On September 5, Lincoln and Halleck allowed McClellan to take an army into the field in response to reports of Rebels invading Maryland. That very day McClellan pushed his forces in the direction of Rockville, Maryland, about 18 miles northwest of Washington.

John Pope's Army of Virginia and the portions of the Army of the Potomac that fought at Second Bull Run fell back into the ring of Washington's fortifications by September 2. This image shows soldiers of the 3rd Massachusetts Heavy Artillery behind the works of Fort Lincoln. (loc)

The army McClellan advanced into the field, the Army of the Potomac, although headed for renown, at that time lacked organization. It was a conglomerate of several different forces, and the men were tired from their recent campaigns. Marching through the picturesque landscape of Maryland, untouched by war compared to Virginia, buoyed their spirits. Nevertheless, raised spirits did not fully diminish or ease the army's marches. Following a march on September 5, a member of the 10th Maine wrote, "I was extremely fatigued and could hardly make my bed."

However, the crisis of the war had come, and the boys in blue were ready to meet it. "The possibilities of a disaster to our arms at this juncture are so momentous that every man feels the necessity of doing his utmost, regardless of all personal considerations," recalled one. They knew the stakes of this campaign.

Turn right out of the parking lot and proceed back to the Seven Corners intersection. Turn right onto Leesburg Pike and make a U-turn in 0.1 miles, onto the Leesburg Pike West. Travel 1.2 miles and turn right onto North Washington Street. Turn left in 0.2 miles onto Great Falls Street. Proceed for 2.9 miles and turn left onto Route 123 S/Dolley Madison Boulevard. Immediately merge right onto the ramp for Route 267 toward Dulles Airport. Drive 0.4 miles and take Exit 18 on the right for I-495 North. Travel 8.8 miles, and keep left on the I-270 North Spur. Stay straight on I-270 North. Drive 2.6 miles and take Exit 6A for Route 28 East toward Rockville. At the end of the ramp, turn right onto Route 28 East. In 0.8 miles, turn left at the stoplight to stay on West Montgomery Avenue. Travel 0.1 miles to turn left on North Adams Street. Take the first left onto West Middle Lane; on the left is the parking lot for the Beall-Dawson House.

Ambrose Burnside's victories in North Carolina earlier in 1862 made him a national hero by the summer of 1862. Abraham Lincoln offered him command of the Army of the Potomac twice before the Maryland Campaign, but Burnside turned down the offer each time. (loc)

GPS: N 39.084700, W 77.155294

STOP 4: BEALL-DAWSON HOUSE, ROCKVILLE

The Army of the Potomac advanced out of Washington and fanned out in several directions to protect various locations threatened by the enemy invasion. "The object of these movements was to feel the enemy—to compel him to develop his intentions—at the same time that the troops were in position readily to cover Baltimore or Washington, to attack him should he hold the line of the Monocacy, or to follow him into Pennsylvania if necessary," wrote George B. McClellan. Conflicting reports of enemy activity also prompted the multi-pronged Federal advance.

To better direct his army, McClellan took to the field personally on September 7. He arrived in Rockville about midnight with "no baggage" and took quarters here at the Beall-Dawson house. McClellan described Mrs. Beall as "an old maid of strong Union sentiment." The commanding general moved his headquarters from the house on September 8.

To cover the several perceived objectives of the Confederate army, McClellan spread out his command over a 16-mile arc north and west of Rockville. He divided his army into wings, each

The Beall-Dawson House dates from 1815 and has hosted prominent visitors throughout its history, including—supposedly—the Marquis de Lafayette during his tour of the United States in 1824. Today, the Montgomery County Historical Society operates it as a house museum. (ro)

Edwin Sumner's army service began in 1819, seven years before his army commander George B. McClellan was born. (loc)

having its own objective, but also keeping close enough together that they could mutually support each other if the need arose.

Major General Ambrose Burnside led the right wing, consisting of the I and IX Corps; the II and XII Corps and Brig. Gen. George Sykes's US Regular Division constituted Maj. Gen. Edwin Sumner's center wing; and Maj. Gen. William Franklin's VI Corps and a division of the IV Corps formed the Army's reserve.

By the night of September 9, McClellan had positioned his force well, but the question remained: what was the enemy doing in Maryland? McClellan's cavalry would have to try to answer that nagging question.

Turn right out of the parking lot and make an immediate right turn on North Adams Street. At the stop sign, turn right onto West Montgomery Avenue, MD-28. Stay on Route 28 for 11.6 miles and turn right into the parking area for the Seneca Creek Greenway Trail. Exit the vehicle and walk along the paved trail running west from the parking lot to its terminus overlooking Seneca Creek.

GPS: N 39.128212, W 77.333123

William Franklin finished first in the 1843 graduating class from West Point. At the beginning of the Civil War, Franklin supervised the construction of the Capitol dome in Washington, DC. (loc)

STOP 5: SENECA CREEK

Though some of these early marches in the campaign were not particularly long or fast-paced, straggling remained a severe problem in the Army of the Potomac. Army headquarters issued an order, on September 9, stressing that such an act "is habitually associated with cowardice, marauding, and theft." Officers were called upon to strictly enforce measures against straggling, and anyone resisting would be doing so "at the risk of death."

Heat also plagued the marches, with the temperature steadily hovering around 80 degrees during the campaign. Dusty roads and tramping feet created an atmosphere so oppressive "that we could scarcely breathe, or even see before us," a New Jersey trooper recorded. The waters of Seneca Creek were a godsend to the men who marched through it.

The friendly inhabitants who greeted the Union men and the lush farmland also made the marching more bearable. "Like the Israelites of old, we looked upon the land, and it was good. The girls no longer made faces at us from the windows, and the people were down at their front gates with cool water . . . . It seemed like Paradise, this Maryland, and many were the blessed damosels [sic] we saw therein," one Maine soldier remembered.

Alfred Pleasonton's performance during the Peninsula Campaign caught the eye of George B. McClellan and earned him command of the Army of the Potomac's cavalry division during the Maryland Campaign. (loc)

Franklin's VI Corps moved through this area and bivouacked here on September 9. Its goal was to guard the army's left and watch the fords on the Potomac. The rest of the army took up a defensive stance on the high ground bordering Seneca Creek to block any enemy movement toward Washington.

Turn right out of the parking lot on Route 28 West, Darnestown Road. In 0.5 miles, take a slight left turn onto Route 107. Travel 4.8 miles into Poolesville; the Civil War Trails sign will be to the right. Pull into the parking lot to read the sign.

GPS: N 39.146098, W 77.416419

STOP 6: POOLESVILLE

Alfred Pleasonton's Yankee cavalrymen were constantly in the saddle those early days of the Maryland Campaign. Beginning on September 2, McClellan ordered the 1st Massachusetts Cavalry to monitor crossing points of the Potomac River and get any information about a Confederate invasion.

Opposing cavalry clashed three separate times in Poolesville during the Maryland Campaign—on September 5, 7, and 8, 1862. (kp)

The Massachusetts men reached Poolesville in the late afternoon of September 5 and proceeded out the other end of town. Soon, they encountered two Virginia cavalry regiments fresh from their river crossing, and the Rebels drove the Bay Staters back into town. The blue-coated horsemen stumbled over obstructions placed in the road by Poolesville's secessionists but managed to make it out of town. In the first cavalry clash of the campaign, the Massachusetts men lost nine wounded and 30 as prisoners while the 3rd and 5th Virginia cavalries suffered three killed and four wounded in their victory.

Federal cavalrymen made a brief foray into Poolesville two days later, and the next day, September 8, they met elements of Col. Thomas Munford's cavalry brigade, which Jeb Stuart sent to expel the enemy from the town. Two artillery pieces accompanied Munford's command.

Munford placed his men and the guns on a stretch of high ground north of Poolesville. His cannon barked away at the Federals, who, in turn, responded with two of their pieces. "I believe that the confounded Yankees can shoot better in the United States than they can when they come to Dixieland," one of the Southern cannoneers remarked. Suddenly, the 3rd Indiana Cavalry burst onto Munford's left, and a fight for the guns ensued. Additional Union troopers almost captured one gun, but the Virginians took it off the field in time. Munford's men fell back to the next defensible position at Monocacy Church. Darkness and a line of dismounted 2nd Virginia cavalrymen ended the Federal pursuit. Overall, Confederate casualties totaled 32 soldiers, compared to 13 Yankees.

Turn right out of the parking lot and make an immediate right onto Route 109, Elgin Road. Drive 2.4 miles and make a left-hand turn on Route 28. The entrance to Monocacy Cemetery is on the left in less than 0.1 miles.

GPS: N 39.180063, W 77.414358

Elon Farnsworth was a 25-year-old captain during the Maryland Campaign. Promoted to brigadier general in the midst of the Gettysburg Campaign, he died during that battle on July 3, 1863. (acab)

The original Monocacy Chapel was constructed in the mid-18th century. A second chapel on the same site was completed by 1760. Its use as a stable by Federal forces during the Civil War destroyed the building. The United Daughters of the Confederacy built the current chapel in 1915. (kp)

STOP 7: BEALLSVILLE/MONOCACY CHURCH

Colonel John Farnsworth's Indiana and Illinois cavalrymen continued pressing Munford's horsemen on the morning of September 9. Finding Munford's Virginians holding the crossroads here at Monocacy Church (present-day Beallsville), John Farnsworth dispatched two companies of the 8th Illinois Cavalry under his nephew Elon to "gain their rear and cut them off." The younger Farnsworth located a desirable pouncing place, and his troopers surged forward into the Confederates. A scuffle ensued, and when one of the Virginians' horses fell—creating an obstacle for the other Confederates involved in the melee—the fight devolved into a rout. The Southern cavaliers "gave way before the determined charge of our men, in doing which some of their horses were shot down, and others falling over these, both men and horses were thrown into heaps," recalled one Illinoisan. "Some escaped through fields and woods, while others were chased and overtaken by our superior horsemen." The gray-clad troopers scattered to the north toward Barnesville.

Leonard Hayes welcomed Thomas Rosser, Wade Hampton, and Fitzhugh Lee to his home for dinner on the night of September 5. The Confederate army did not always receive such a warm welcome from Marylanders throughout the campaign. Today, the home is privately owned. Please respect the privacy of the owners. (kp)

Without losing a single man or beast, the Illinoisans inflicted about a dozen casualties and captured the flag of the 12th Virginia Cavalry. This critical crossroads, bearing the east-west road from Rockville to the Monocacy and the north-south route from the Potomac to Hyattstown, now belonged to Pleasonton's troopers.

Exit to the right out of Monocacy Cemetery, and turn left onto Route 109, Beallsville Road. Travel 3.6 miles before turning left on Barnesville Road. Immediately after the left-hand turn, you will pass the Hayes House on the left, where several Confederate commanders dined during their stay in Barnesville. In 0.2 miles, pull into the parking lot of St. Mary's Catholic Church on the left. There, find a Civil War Trails sign.

GPS: N 39.221199, W 77.381423

STOP 8: BARNESVILLE

Federal troopers poured north, pursuing their adversaries on the road toward Barnesville on September 9. They quickly dashed into town here, captured all the Confederate videttes posted in the village, and continued the running fight all the way to the base of Sugarloaf Mountain, several miles distant. There, a bold stand by W. H. F. "Rooney" Lee kept the mountaintop's revealing vistas out of the hands of the Federals.

In these multiple running fights on September 9, the Federals did not record a single casualty while the Confederates lost four killed, five wounded, and 27 captured.

Despite the small stature of these cavalry fights, they did have consequences on the campaign. First, they showed that Union cavalrymen could fight toe to toe with the enemy and come out on top. "Thus far my cavalry have gained the advantage," McClellan informed Halleck. Also, the advances made by the Army of the Potomac on September 9 put its lead elements within a long day's march from Frederick. All of this came on the same day that Robert E. Lee issued Special Orders No. 191, dividing his army into several portions. Lee believed he had a large cushion of time to carry out his investment of the Union garrisons in the Shenandoah Valley. Part of this false sense of security resulted from poor intelligence work by Major General Stuart, who failed to keep his commander apprised of the Federal advances despite being within earshot of the fighting on September 9. Lee's belief that he had more time than he did to carry out the provisions of Special Orders 191 would prove nearly disastrous.

Turn right out of the parking lot, and drive 0.2 miles. Turn left onto Route 109, now called Old Hundred Road. Travel 5.7 miles into Hyattstown. Turn right onto Route 355 South. In less than 0.1 miles, turn left into the parking lot of the Hyattstown Volunteer Fire Department. Exit your car and walk to the Civil War Trails sign.

GPS: N 39.279938, W 77.314739

STOP 9: HYATTSTOWN

Jeb Stuart's cavalry screen stretched from east of Frederick in an arc southwest to the Potomac River early in the campaign. Wade Hampton's Southern Brigade manned the center of the line at Hyattstown, a small town along the road from Washington and Rockville to Frederick.

A Union reconnaissance to this town on the evening of September 8 broke up Stuart's "Sabers and Roses Ball" in Urbana (see Chapter 1, Stop 13). By the time Stuart himself arrived on the scene, the Federal threat had diminished.

Once again on September 9, Yankee cavalrymen charged into the town but failed to take it. The fight for Hyattstown did not conclude until two days later.

By September 11, with Lee's army pulling out of Frederick and moving west, Stuart abandoned his advanced line to consolidate his cavalry screen closer to the city. Federal infantry of the II Corps arrived near Hyattstown by mid-afternoon and cleared the town of its Rebel occupants. "[L]ine of battle was formed . . . deployed as skirmishers, and advanced to the woods in our front," remembered one participant. Two batteries of Union guns opened fire in response to their Confederate counterparts, but the line of blue "was then advanced, and dislodged" the enemy.

Having advanced on several fronts, the Army of the Potomac now lay within a dozen miles of Frederick.

Exit the parking lot turning right onto Route 355. Travel 0.7 miles and turn right onto Route 75, Green Valley Road. Drive 4.8 miles before turning right onto Fingerboard Road, Route 80. In 2.9 miles, make a left-hand turn onto Penn Shop Road. Travel 3.1 miles before turning left onto Route 27, Ridge Road. In 1 mile, use the second from the left lane to turn left onto East Ridgeville Boulevard.

GPS: N 39.364506, W 77.161115

STOP 10: PARR'S RIDGE

George McClellan's first defensive position in the campaign rested behind the waters of Seneca Creek, but he next focused on the high ground of Parr's Ridge, an 830-foot rise of earth—the highest elevation between Baltimore and the Catoctin Mountains—along the National Road. Today, despite modern development, the view to the west from this high ground clearly explains why McClellan coveted such a place to counter any Confederate offensives.

The view from Parr's Ridge shows almost the entire valley, from the ridge all the way to the Catoctin Mountains, visible in the distance, on the west side of Frederick. (kp)

Soldiers of the Union IX Corps under Brig. Gen. Jesse Reno crested the ridge on the army's right on September 11, securing the road to Baltimore. By this date, McClellan had evidence of Confederates moving west from Frederick, yet an uncertainty remained as to the enemy's plans. "This uncertainty as to the intentions of the enemy obliged me . . . to march cautiously," he admitted. But the simultaneous capture of Parr's Ridge and Sugarloaf Mountain on September 11 provided McClellan with some extra pluck. When he received confirmation of the enemy's abandonment of Frederick the next day, he ordered his troops to move quickly on that city. "It was now determined to move more rapidly," recalled IX Corps division commander Jacob Cox, "and early in the morning of the 12th I was ordered to march to New Market and thence to Frederick."

Exit to the right out of the parking lot onto East Ridgeville Boulevard. Stay straight on East Ridgeville Boulevard, which eventually becomes Route 144, Old National Pike. In 6.4 miles, pull over at the Civil War Trails sign in the center of New Market on the right side of the road. Note: This Civil War Trails sign is for the Gettysburg Campaign.

GPS: N 39.382970, W 77.271122

STOP 11: NEW MARKET

The Army of the Potomac's right wing—Hooker's I Corps and Reno's IX Corps—passed through New Market on their September 12 march, destined for Frederick.

One of Reno's troops remembered the movement as "painfully laborious" in the morning rain. Another recalled a more pleasant scene of four young ladies greeting the soldiers with "a Beautiful New flag of the Stripes & Stars & with a beautiful Bow of ribbons of read [sic], white & blue on the top of the flag staff." He concluded: "New Market is a fine little town."

Fitzhugh Lee's Virginia cavalry brigade had been stationed in New Market earlier in the campaign, and Federal intelligence sources indicated Stonewall Jackson established his headquarters in the town (this information turned out to be false). The arriving Union soldiers did not find the enemy in New Market, although local citizens presented them with information that the Confederate army recently in Frederick had left in a westerly direction. Armed with this news, Jacob Cox's all-Ohio Kanawha Division—in the van of Reno's column—continued marching toward Frederick.

Continue straight on Old National Pike, Route 144. Travel 6.4 miles. Just after crossing over Interstate 70, turn right onto East Patrick Street. Make an immediate right turn into the parking lot. Exit the vehicle to walk to the Jug Bridge monument.

GPS: N 39.404754, W 77.383212

Rain accompanied the Federal march to New Market, "making the march painfully laborious," recalled one Union soldier. "The roads became so slippery that it was with difficulty that the men could keep on their feet." (kp)

STOP 12: JUG BRIDGE

As the Army of Northern Virginia vacated its camps in Frederick on September 10, Jeb Stuart constricted his cavalry line tighter to the city. Wade Hampton held a line at the Jug Bridge, which carried the National Road over the Monocacy River. Three guns and a squadron of the 2nd South Carolina Cavalry constituted Hampton's defense against what he knew to be an enemy in "heavy force" advancing on his position. When Jacob Cox's oncoming Federals came into view on the east side of the river at approximately 2:00 p.m. on September 12, Hampton's guns opened fire.

Jacob Cox unlimbered his artillery to counter the Confederates (and killed two men) from the higher ground east of the Monocacy. With Union artillery distracting the Confederate gunners, Cox sent two infantry brigades to carry the bridge. Colonel Augustus Moor's Ohio brigade charged directly across the span while the 30th Ohio forded the river to the north, hoping to flank the Rebel defenders. Once the Unionists came across the bridge, Hampton started to pull back, slowly withdrawing to the other side of Frederick.

At the start of the Civil War, Wade Hampton reportedly owned more land than anyone else in the Confederacy. He equipped his own unit at the war's outset and became a reliable commander for the Confederate army throughout the Civil War, despite his lack of military training. (loc)

The men of the Kanawha division deployed into battle formations and began following the Confederate legions around 5:00 p.m. Colonel Moor rode at the head of the advance, along with the Chicago Dragoons and a single piece of artillery. A rogue Union staff officer rode alongside the column, proclaiming it moved too slowly. He wondered why, as the enemy had completely evacuated Frederick, he believed. Moor heard those words, took offense to them, and spurred his entourage forward. At a point where the road into downtown Frederick made a turn, Hampton's rearguard pounced on the Federals. Moor's men unlimbered a gun and fired into Frederick's "crowded streets," an act that Hampton called an "unparalleled atrocity," while the Confederate cavalrymen charged toward Moor's party. The fight was over almost as soon as it began. Hampton's troopers captured Moor despite attempts by the 11th Ohio Infantry to save their brigade commander. While "the carbine smoke and the smell of powder still lingered," Hampton's brigade withdrew west of Frederick to a position atop Catoctin Mountain as the van of the Army of the Potomac entered the east side of Frederick.

Builder Leonard Harbaugh planted this stone jug on the bridge he built, thus giving the Jug Bridge its distinctive name. Harbaugh's bridge no longer stands, but the stone jug sits in a park not far from the bridge site. (ro)

Turn left out of the parking area onto East Patrick Street, Route 144. In 0.3 miles, turn left onto Monocacy Boulevard. Travel 0.9 miles and use the left two lanes

The Jug Bridge derived its name from the stone "demijohn" that sat on the east side of the bridge. It was constructed in 1808. The bridge abutments still stand on either side of the Monocacy River. (loc)

to turn left onto South East Street. Drive 0.4 miles on Route 85 before turning left onto Route 355 South. Travel 1.9 miles. Turn right into the Best Farm, a part of Monocacy National Battlefield. Continue driving on the dirt road to reach a parking area. There, several interpretive exhibits relate to the Maryland Campaign.

GPS: N 39.370532, W 77.398792

STOP 13: BEST FARM

The bulk of the Army of the Potomac did not arrive around Frederick until September 13. Several 27th Indiana soldiers, deployed as skirmishers in front of the XII Corps, around noon stumbled upon a package on the southeast edge of Frederick. Corporal Barton W. Mitchell retrieved the package, opened it, and found some paper with three cigars enclosed. Mitchell passed the find to his sergeant, John M. Bloss, who read the document and began to recognize its importance—a lost copy of Lee's Special Orders No. 191. The "Lost Orders" quickly worked its way up the chain of command until it came into George B. McClellan's hands.

While Mitchell's discovery has been hailed by many as a great intelligence coup "the all-time military jackpot," proclaimed one historian—it did not explain every bit of the blurry intelligence picture McClellan faced. The document made Lee's intentions clear, to be sure, and clarified that his army was moving in two diverging directions, but were the orders real or a set-up by some Confederates? Usually, McClellan "would take it as a ruse de guerre," wrote one of his former enemies after the war, "but it seems that General McClellan gave it his confidence." This blurry piece of intelligence also failed to clarify the size of the Army of Northern Virginia, and some of its contents differed with the information McClellan had received from other sources. Additionally, the copy of Special Orders No. 191 that McClellan read began with Paragraph III. What information did Paragraphs I and II contain that McClellan had no clear way to discover?

Thus, McClellan's first move needed to verify that Lee's forces remained divided and that Lee's army still implemented the four-day-old orders (Lee dictated the orders on September 9, but they reached McClellan in the afternoon of September

Traditionally, history has said that Cpl. Barton W. Mitchell stumbled upon the lost copy of Special Orders No. 191 in the area of Robert E. Lee's former headquarters near the Best Farm. Mitchell was 46 at the time of his discovery. He survived a leg wound at Antietam, but it plagued him for the rest of his life. He died in 1868. (kp)

13). Upon confirmation from his cavalry chief Alfred Pleasonton that the situation reflected in the "Lost Orders" held true, General McClellan crafted a plan to defeat the Rebel army in detail and liberate the Harpers Ferry garrison. With the stage thus set for the next phase of the campaign, the initiative Robert E. Lee had fought so hard to gain in the war's Eastern Theater was quickly slipping from his grasp.

Other evidence strongly supports the theory that Barton W. Mitchell found the "Lost Orders" near Frederick's southeast corner. Unfortunately, the site is an industrial park today, but can still be visited: N 39.407924, W 77.396581. (kp)

The "Lost Orders" can now be found in George B. McClellan's papers at the Library of Congress. It is still the subject of much debate today: when was it found and how important was it really? (loc)

Battle of Harpers Ferry

CHAPTER THREE

This route follows portions of the Army of Northern Virginia from Frederick, Maryland, to Harpers Ferry, West Virginia. The route follows both infantry and cavalry and will highlight notable locations associated with the siege and capitulation of Harpers Ferry on September 15, 1862. The routes of Jackson and McLaws are featured.

Lee set his army in motion on September 10. The four parts of the Army of Northern Virginia all had specific instructions about where to go and what to do. Lee assigned the most important task to Stonewall Jackson's command with assistance from the divisions of Brig. Gen. John G. Walker and Maj. Gen. Lafayette McLaws. Working in concert, these commanders would approach Harpers Ferry from three different directions. From the west Jackson would clear the garrison at Martinsburg, then move toward Harpers Ferry as the hammer. McLaws and Walker would serve as the anvil, with McLaws scaling Maryland Heights to the northeast of Harpers Ferry and Walker advancing on Loudoun Heights to the southeast. The Federals would either be captured, defeated or forced to pull out with the threat of the Confederates encircling them.

Lee, wrongfully, assumed the Federals in Martinsburg and Harpers Ferry could be dealt with quickly. He expected the Confederates assigned to the Harpers Ferry expedition to return to the main army in Hagerstown by September

Today Harpers Ferry attracts not only history buffs but also nature seekers with its river recreation, hiking and scenic vistas. (kp)

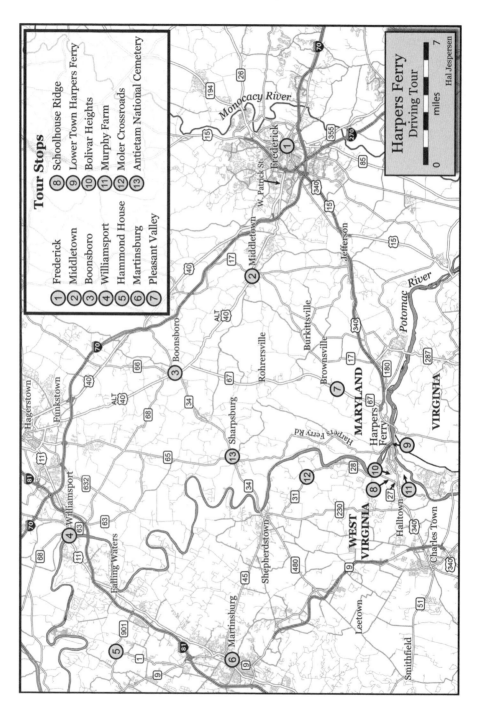

HARPERS FERRY DRIVING TOUR—This portion of the driving tour will follow the route of the Confederates to Harpers Ferry, West Virginia, from Frederick, Maryland. Jackson, for various reasons, fell behind the timetable Lee set for him to remove the Federals from Martinsburg and Harpers Ferry. This had a strategic impact on Lee's plans at Sharpsburg.

12-13. Both of Lee's top commanders, Stonewall Jackson and James Longstreet, disagreed with Lee's plan and thought it risky. To divide the army in the face of the Army of the Potomac welcomed disaster, but Lee wanted to reestablish his supply and communication lines through the Shenandoah Valley as soon as possible. Already, stragglers and supplies concentrated at Winchester for a movement north to Lee.

Today, Frederick is one of the largest cities in Maryland. The revived downtown maintains its original character with historic sites and museums, such as the National Museum of Civil War Medicine. (kp)

After making the plans with Jackson for the movement on Harpers Ferry, Lee shared the plan with Longstreet. Still opposed to Lee's strategy, Longstreet later wrote, "it seemed useless for me to offer any further opposition." Longstreet did convince Lee to send more men with McLaws, specifically to include the division of Maj. Gen. Richard H. Anderson.

On the morning of September 10, Jackson's and McLaws's columns marched west out of Frederick. Simultaneously, Walker's division marched south toward the Monocacy Aqueduct, then to Cheek's Ford to re-cross back into Virginia. Little did Lee know but time was of the essence: McClellan moved west with unexpected aggressiveness. Creating more challenge, the forces in Martinsburg and Harpers Ferry were larger than Lee estimated. The final challenge to Lee's plan developed in the next few days: McClellan would have in his hands Special Orders 191. When McClellan read the orders, they were four days old, but Lee's army was still divided—it had not completed the missions and reconnected at Hagerstown.

One of the most iconic images of Confederate soldiers during the war, this rare image shows portions of the Army of Northern Virginia in column waiting to move through downtown Frederick in September 1862, although some historians believe it to be in 1864. (Historical Society of Frederick, Maryland.)

As the Confederates under Stonewall Jackson entered Middletown on September 10, local resident Nancy Crouse was flying a large US flag from her balcony. Confederates entered the house to remove the flag and, legend has it, found Crouse wrapped in her flag. She stated, "You may shoot me, but never will I willingly give up my country's flag into the hands of traitors." This story may be the basis of the Barbara Fritchie myth in Frederick. (ro)

Start the tour at the National Museum of Civil War Medicine, located at 42 East Patrick Street. Several Civil War Trails markers near here tell the story of Frederick during the Civil War. Three markers are attached to the west wall of the museum while one marker of note is located at the northeast corner of the Market and Patrick streets intersection.

GPS: N 39.414018, W 77.409297

STOP 1: FREDERICK

As the second largest city in Maryland, Frederick's citizens were on edge during the Confederate occupation. Lee sought to alleviate townspeople's fears by encamping his men outside of city limits. On September 10, large portions of Lee's army marched through town. Citizens turned out to see their "ragged" foes. The lead elements of Brig. Gen. John R. Jones's division began their march around 3:00 a.m., followed by Lawton's and A. P. Hill's divisions. However, due to Jackson and Hill's disagreement in Dranesville, Hill still journeyed under arrest while Lawrence Branch led Hill's men.

The soldiers teased the Yankee-leaning locals in town. A Confederate band struck up "The Girl I Left Behind Me," and many Confederates flirted with local women along the streets. Most civilian loyalty was not in question, though, as one Confederate wrote, "it was not difficult to discern that this enthusiasm was roused only for display." Jackson himself had some fun, trying to confuse the locals on his destination as he openly called for Chambersburg maps from his chief engineer, James Boswell.

It took the Confederates many hours to pass through Frederick's streets, and at times, the men stood in column to wait for other units ahead to clear. At one of these times in mid-morning, a photographer took a rare image of Confederate infantry. It is only one of a handful of photographs showing Confederate infantry under arms. After Jackson's men cleared Frederick (Jackson had the longest route of the three columns to Harpers Ferry via Williamsport, Maryland), the enlarged division under Lafayette McLaws went next. Longstreet's men then followed, heading for Boonsboro. The Federals trailed only two days behind.

Take East Patrick Street to West Patrick Street (go through the intersection with Market Street). Continue for 0.5 mile after Market Street and bear left to remain on West Patrick Street. Continue for 2.2 miles and take a left onto Alternate Route 40 (Old National Pike). Stay on Alternate Route 40 for 5 miles and take a left onto South Church Street. The Civil War Trails sign for Middletown will be on the left, located at 12 South Church Street (parking lot for the Christ Reformed Church).

GPS: N 39.443886, W 77.547905

STOP 2: MIDDLETOWN

Middletown unabashedly supported the Union. As the Confederates entered the town on September 10, they were clearly not welcomed. Henry Kyd Douglas, one of Jackson's staff members, told this story: "As Gen. Thomas J. Stonewall Jackson rode through Middletown on September 10, two very pretty girls with ribbons of red, white, and blue in their hair and small Union flags in their hands ran out to the curbstone, and laughingly waved

Maj. Gen. Lafayette McLaws was a rising star in the Army of Northern Virginia by the time of the Maryland Campaign. Many historians believed Lee was grooming him for a possible corps or wing command. (loc)

The first federally funded road project, the National Road was begun under the administration of Thomas Jefferson; and expanded east to Baltimore and west to St. Louis. The road incorporated other smaller segments that were used to travel westward. Today, Route Alt. 40 and Route 40 follow original traces of this road. (kp)

their colors defiantly in the face of the General. He bowed and lifted his cap with a quiet smile and said to his staff, 'We evidently have no friends in this town.'" Many believe this may be the basis of the Barbara Fritchie legend in Frederick. The story of a defiant Unionist woman standing up to Stonewall was made famous in the poem "Barbara Fritchie," by John Greenleaf Whittier, which took on a life of its own despite no factual evidence that an encounter between Fritchie and Jackson ever occurred.

Once Jackson's men cleared the center of town, McLaws's column turned south onto South Church Street and marched in front of this location from right to left. Its route went to Burkittsville, then across South Mountain, and on to Pleasant Valley, ultimately reaching Maryland Heights. McLaws's men had the shortest route of the three columns to Harpers Ferry but the most difficult mission. They not only had to gain the steep and rugged terrain of Maryland Heights through battle, but McLaws was also forced to leave some men behind him at South Mountain to protect his rear from the Federals and leave other men along the Potomac River to block the enemy's escape route. Longstreet recognized the importance of McLaws's mission and convinced Lee to assign three brigades of infantry under Brig. Gen. Cadmus M. Wilcox to McLaws, an addition to the brigades under Maj. Gen. Richard H. Anderson added days before. In total, McLaws now commanded nearly 10,000 men, almost a quarter of the Army of Northern Virginia.

Several notable Civil War-related buildings remain in town (all are privately owned, so please respect the privacy of the owners while viewing the structures from the outside). The Crouse house is located at 204 West Main Street. Here, Nancy Crouse stood up to marching Confederates when they tried to take down her US flag. (See Chapter 4's Tour Stop 3 for more information about Middletown's Civil War era buildings.)

Turn right out of the parking lot and then left onto West Main Street. Continue west on Alternate Route 40 for 6.2 miles. The white house to the left is the Murdock house. Here, Maj. Gen. Stonewall Jackson made his headquarters on September 10, 1862. Henry Kyd Douglas claimed Jackson was nearly captured here by a Federal cavalry patrol from Harpers Ferry. Continue for 1.5 miles. A Civil War Trails marker stands on the left, at the corner of North Main Street and Shafer Park Drive.

GPS: N 39.509785, W 77.654042

STOP 3: BOONSBORO

Stonewall Jackson reached Boonsboro around 10:00 a.m., on September 10, and set up his

The historic Murdock House still stands along the National Turnpike east of Boonsboro. Jackson's headquarters was probably across the road from the house. (kp)

headquarters east of town near the Murdock house. Thus far Jackson had made great time since leaving Frederick. His men had traveled nearly fourteen miles and over two mountain ranges (Catoctin Mountain and South Mountain), though only J. R. Jones's division made it to the west side of South Mountain via Turner's Gap. Jackson's other two divisions were still east of Turner's Gap. Many Antietam historians have debated why Jackson stopped his march west so early on September 10, uncommon for a commander known for his fast marches. One theory suggests he possibly delayed his movement to confuse the Federals on his future route of march.

Jackson seemed to take his time to reconnoiter various routes to Martinsburg. Now a macadamized road stretched before him, ideal for marching. From Boonsboro, he determined to continue on the National Pike and then take a direct macadamized road to Williamsport, where he could cross the Potomac River back into Virginia and proceed to Martinsburg. Though Williamsport lay further west than Jackson originally intended to march, he believed it would be an easier march since the road was mostly paved.

In the afternoon, Jackson sent his escort/guard, the 4th Virginia cavalry, north toward Hagerstown to check out a report of Federal cavalry in the area. In the meantime, the Union 1st Maryland Potomac

Home Brigade Cavalry scouted from Harpers Ferry northward on the Sharpsburg Road toward Boonsboro. According to Henry Kyd Douglas, a dozen or so Federal cavalry approached Jackson's location near the Murdock house. Alerted by his staff, he mounted his horse and galloped eastward. Soon, the 4th Virginia cavalry returned to Boonsboro and forced the Marylanders southward back toward Sharpsburg.

Located seven miles west of Martinsburg, the old B&O Railroad still runs through North Mountain Depot. Jackson decided to cut the railroad here to block any Federal retreat west from Martinsburg via the railroad and to further isolate the Federal forces in the lower Valley. Confederates under A. P. Hill heated the rails and twisted them around trees along the tracks. (kp)

Though one of the more famous events of the campaign, Jackson's other staff members disputed this account after the war. Federal cavalry's appearance from the south may have convinced Jackson that the best route to Martinsburg was not south through Sharpsburg but northwest to Williamsport. Then Jackson could either defeat the Federals at Martinsburg or force them eastward to Harpers Ferry.

Continue west on Alternate Route 40 for 0.8 mile and take a left onto Route 68 (Lappans Road). Travel for 11.1 miles (the road will turn into Route 63, then Conococheague Street). Take a left onto West Potomac Street and travel for 0.2 mile, then turn right into the Chesapeake and Ohio Canal National Historical Park Visitor Center parking lot. The Civil War Trails marker, facing the Potomac River, stands on the canal towpath. Various historic markers in this area pertain to the history of Williamsport and the canal.

GPS: N 39.600840, W 77.827626

STOP 4: WILLIAMSPORT

The Potomac River crossings here became a popular spot for armies on both sides to wade the river. Nearby, Light's Ford allowed travelers along the Valley Road (modern day Route 11) to cross between Maryland and Virginia. Lemen's Ferry served as a cable ferry and operated here before and during the war.

Following a twelve-mile march from Boonsboro, Jackson's column arrived in Williamsport after sunrise on September 11. Although his men made good time, his march to Williamsport added eleven miles to his originally planned route. Jackson's men quickly crossed at Light's Ford and continued southward for ten miles toward Martinsburg.

Turn right out of the parking lot onto Route 11 south (Williamsport Pike) and cross over the Potomac River. Travel for 3 miles and take the right exit for Interstate 81 south. Continue south on Interstate 81 for 3 miles and take Exit 20, turn right onto Route 901 (Hammonds Mill Road). Travel 2.3 miles and make a left to remain on Route 901 (Hammonds Mill Road). In 0.2 miles, the Civil War Trails marker for the Hammond house will be on the right.

GPS: N 39.558583, W 77.953243

STOP 5: HAMMOND HOUSE

Once Jackson learned that Brig. Gen. Julius White still occupied Martinsburg, he divided his force to cast a wide net to prevent the Federals from fleeing westward or northward. His first objective focused on North Mountain Depot, just two miles west of the Hammond house. By capturing the small Federal force there, Jackson cut the B&O Railroad and closed off a possible escape route for White's men. With A. P. Hill's division north of Martinsburg and Confederate cavalry sent south of Martinsburg, White had only one direction to escape, east to Harpers Ferry. Jackson made his headquarters at the Hammond House and allowed

The Hammond House was originally built in 1838 but burned down in 1978. The current structure is a modern reconstruction using some of the original brick walls. Stonewall Jackson was one of many Civil War generals to use the house as a headquarters. (kp)

his men to go into camp. They had marched nearly twenty-three miles, with many dropping out along the way due to exhaustion.

That night, as Jackson's men slept, White evacuated Martinsburg. The next day, September 12, arrived—the date specified in Special Orders 191 for Jackson to complete his mission.

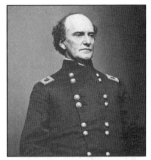

Drive straight from the Civil War Trails marker and take a left onto Route 1 (Harlan Springs Road). Continue for 3.8 miles and take a left onto Route 9 (Hedgesville Road). Travel 3.7 miles (Route 9 becomes Queen Street as it enters Martinsburg) and make a left onto East Martin Street. Travel two blocks and make a left into the Martinsburg Train Station. The Civil War Trails marker, facing the Roundhouse, will be on the right in the parking lot.

GPS: N 39.458892, W 77.960883

Brig. Gen. Julius White had an interesting career during the Civil War. After the Maryland Campaign, a court of inquiry acquitted him for his actions at Harpers Ferry. He led a division in the Knoxville Campaign, then was sent back east with Burnside and served as his chief of staff through the battle of the Crater. He continued to serve with the IX Corps until it was disbanded, then White resigned from the military. (loc)

STOP 6: MARTINSBURG

By 1862, most facilities in Martinsburg that supported the railroad had been destroyed, and Confederates routinely threatened or attacked the trains and tracks. The current roundhouse here was built in 1866 to replace a similar structure Stonewall Jackson destroyed in 1861.

The best view of Harpers Ferry is from Maryland Heights. A strenuous but worthwhile hike leads you past the Naval Battery and gives you a great perspective of the confluence of the Potomac and Shenandoah rivers. (kp)

One of the geographic beauties of Harpers Ferry is the "double water gap," where the Shenandoah and Potomac Rivers converge and cut through two mountain ranges. The feature allowed for the industrial rise of the region using water power, but the mountain ranges made the town nearly impossible to defend militarily. (kp)

Brig. Gen. William Barksdale was a proud Mississippian who served in Congress before the war. Once Mississippi seceded, he joined the state militia and then rose to command a brigade in the Army of Northern Virginia. His men were known as good fighters and some of the best troops in Lee's army. (loc)

Jackson cautiously approached Martinsburg from the northwest as he awaited word from his cavalry to determine if the Federals had evacuated the town. Entering the town in mid-morning, the Confederates received a hero's welcome. Unlike the towns in Maryland, Martinsburg sympathized with the Confederate cause. White had beaten a hasty retreat to the southeast to join the Federal garrison at Harpers Ferry; his 3,000 men had left a lot of government stores and property behind.

Although known for his forced marches, on this day, Jackson encamped his men just to the east of Martinsburg, after moving an average nine miles from their starting points that morning. Jackson sent a message to Lee about his progress. He planned to head toward Harpers Ferry to coordinate with McLaws's and Walker's forces to surround Harpers Ferry. This would be a difficult task. Geographic features did not allow for easy communication between the three Confederate columns. Jackson had cleared the Federals from Martinsburg, but his objective to remove the garrison at Harpers Ferry still remained.

Turn right out of the parking lot onto East Martin Street. In two blocks, make a left onto North Queen Street (Route 9 south). Travel 1.3 miles and make a right turn onto the exit for Route 9 east. Travel on Route 9 for 13.6 miles and take the right exit for Route 340 east (make a left at the top of the exit ramp to turn onto Route 340 east). Travel west on Route 340 for 8.8 miles (passing Harpers Ferry) and take the right exit for Route 67 north. Continue on Route 67 north for 3.4 miles and make a right into the parking lot for the Brownsville Church of the Brethren. The Civil Was Trails sign is near the exit for the parking lot on the north side of the church.

GPS: N 39.368951, W 77.670171

STOP 7: PLEASANT VALLEY

From the spot where the Civil War Trails marker stands, Maryland Heights/Elk Ridge rises to the front. Harpers Ferry is off to the left, and it was here that Col. Dixon Miles sent Col. Thomas Ford to defend the important heights. Rising 1,400 feet above sea level, Maryland Heights was the key to Harpers Ferry: whoever commanded Maryland Heights commanded the town since that height dominated all the other heights around Harpers Ferry—Loudoun Heights, Bolivar Heights and Camp Hill.

Beginning on September 11, Confederates under Major General McLaws arrived here in Pleasant Valley. Lee gave McLaws a large force (nearly 10,000 men), reflective of the importance of his mission. Their goal was to take Maryland Heights and then coordinate with Brigadier General Walker (who was supposed to take

Part of one of the richest families in South Carolina, Brig. Gen. Joseph Kershaw was a lawyer and state politician before the war. He assumed command of a brigade in the Army of Northern Virginia in February 1862. This was after General P. G. T. Beauregard called him a "militia idiot" after the battle of First Manassas. (phcw)

The saddle in the mountains is Solomon's Gap. Here, Confederate forces under Barksdale and Kershaw accessed Maryland Heights. Using a cart patch, thousands of Confederates slowly climbed the heights and headed south towards Harpers Ferry. (kp)

Though a Virginian by birth, Col. Thomas Ford detested slavery and moved to Ohio where he became a self-studied lawyer. He did serve a short time in the Mexican War, but Ford was more of a politician than a lawyer or a soldier: he served as lieutenant governor of Ohio and a Republican party activist. (cbhrco)

A man much blamed for the disaster at Harpers Ferry, Col. Dixon Miles has been called incompetent, a fool, and a drunk. A native Marylander and a graduate of West Point in 1824, Miles served in several posts in the US Army, including in the Mexican War and fighting Indians in the west. He commanded a division at the battle of First Bull Run but was in reserve near Centreville. He was accused of drunkenness and reassigned to protect the B&O Railroad in March 1862. (loc)

Loudoun Heights) and Jackson, coming in from the west from Martinsburg. The three columns would surround Harpers Ferry to force the evacuation of the garrison or its surrender.

The saddle formation along the heights directly in front of this location is Solomon's Gap. Here on September 12, Brig. Gen. William Barksdale's and Brig. Gen. Joseph Kershaw's brigades accessed the crest of the ridge. The Confederates cleared a small force of Federals near the gap and then marched south (to the left) for four miles. McLaws faced limitations when choosing whom he could commit to capturing Maryland Heights by advancing along the narrow spine on the heights. He wanted to use the bulk of his force to block off the Pleasant Valley to prevent any Federals in Harpers Ferry from escaping northward through the valley. By the early morning of September 13, the Confederates confronted Ford's Federal brigade along the crest of Maryland Heights, about a half mile from Harpers Ferry. Most of Ford's men were new to warfare, and they had just recently been brigaded together. Additionally, Colonel Miles, Union commander at Harpers Ferry, had been previously ordered to build strong earthworks and a blockhouse atop Maryland Heights, but by September 13, only slight breastworks and a field of abatis protected his men.

As the sun rose on September 13, Kershaw's South Carolinians began pushing their way through and around the field of abatis. Barksdale moved his Mississippians down the eastern slope of Elk Ridge, attempting to skirt the Federal position. As

Lt. Nicholas DeGraff of the 115th New York wrote, "this morning opened with the boom of cannon and the crash of musketry and we were soon convinced that it was not a fourth of July celebration." Ford had requested artillery, but Miles had denied his request, leaving Ford's men outnumbered and outgunned. Ford's untested 126th New York held its ground and represented itself well. Around 10:30 a.m., Col. Eliakim Sherrill of the 126th New York went down with a jaw wound, and the regiment began to break. Also, at about this time, some of Barksdale's Mississippians found their way around the Federal rear and opened fire. After several hours of a stout defense, the Federals started to flee the heights.

On the southern slope, Ford had established his headquarters at the Naval Battery. Constructed earlier in the year, this battery position helped to defend the Camp Hill area from attack. Ford and Miles worked hard to rally the Federals as they retreated down the slope past the Naval Battery. The Federals established a new line about a quarter mile from their original breastworks (now held by Kershaw's and Barksdale's Confederates). Miles decided the situation was stable and headed back to Harpers Ferry. This proved a costly mistake when, several hours later, Ford ordered his men to fall back to Harpers Ferry. Though the Federals regrouped and the Confederates waited, Ford believed his line was shattered and ordered his men off the heights. When Miles learned of Ford's decision, he yelled, "What does that mean? They are coming down! Hell and damnation!" With Maryland Heights given up and the simultaneous arrival of Walker and Jackson, the Confederates completely encircled Harpers Ferry. Brigadier General White (commander of the former garrison

Named for a small stone schoolhouse located near Route 340, Schoolhouse Ridge was used by Stonewall Jackson's forces as a way to close the trap on the Federals in Harpers Ferry. The ridge parallels the Federal position along Bolivar Heights. The ridge was preserved and included in the National Park in 2004. (kp)

Benjamin Grimes Davis, a Southerner by birth, was a West Point graduate and remained loyal to the Union when the war broke out. He became a colonel of the 8th New York Cavalry in June 1862. He became quickly frustrated with Colonel Miles in Harpers Ferry. Davis was killed in action at the battle of Brandy Station a year later. (loc)

at Martinsburg, now Miles's second in command) argued to withdraw from Harpers Ferry after the loss of Maryland Heights. Miles refused, reportedly saying, "I am ordered to hold this place and God damn my soul to hell if I don't."

After the fighting on Maryland Heights, McLaws moved the bulk of his infantry off Maryland Heights to face the new Federal threat north of him in Pleasant Valley. With the Federal victory at Crampton's Gap on September 14, the Federal VI Corps under Maj. Gen. William Franklin poured through the gap into Pleasant Valley. McLaws lined up his force across Pleasant Valley near Brownsville. He used the terrain to hide his small force, and his ruse worked as Franklin (who was ordered by McClellan to move south to relieve the Federal garrison at Harpers Ferry) wrote to McClellan that the Confederate force in front of him outnumbered his corps. Thus, sealed in Harpers Ferry, the Federals faced an unhappy fate.

To see related sites in nearby Brownsville, refer to Stop 10 in Chapter Four.

To continue to Stop 8:

Here on Shenandoah Street, the 1,400 Union cavalry under Col. Benjamin Grimes Davis lined up on the evening of September 14. Crossing the Potomac River on the pontoon bridge, Davis led the column around the base of Maryland Heights and north along the Harpers Ferry-Sharpsburg Road. During the successful escape, the cavalry captured a Confederate ammunition train near Williamsport, Maryland, that comprised of 80 wagons and 300 horses and mules. (kp)

Turn left onto Route 67 south. Almost immediately after resuming the drive, take note of the Yarrowsburg Road to the right. Kershaw's and Barksdale's brigades used portions of this road to reach Solomon's Gap. Drive 2.7 miles to the right exit for Route 340 west. Remain on Route 340 for 5 miles and turn right onto Route 27 (Bakerton Road). In 0.7 miles make a left into the National Park Service parking lot for Schoolhouse Ridge North.

GPS: N 39.325558, W 77.766914

STOP 8: SCHOOLHOUSE RIDGE

In 1862, most of this area had been cleared of trees, especially the area across the road on Bolivar Heights. When Jackson arrived here on the morning of September 13, he heard the fighting up on Maryland Heights. He had had little communication up to that point with Walker or McLaws, and with the Federal garrison between the three commands, communication remained difficult.

On the morning of September 13, Jackson knew White's Federals had moved east from Martinsburg to join the Federal garrison at Harpers Ferry. This brought the garrison's strength to nearly 14,000.

Maryland Heights dominates the town of Harpers Ferry and the US Armory along the Potomac River. It is easy to see why the control of the heights was so important to the survival of any military force in the town. (loc)

Picked by George Washington as a location of a Federal armory for the new national government in 1794, Harpers Ferry already enjoyed prosperity from the power of the two rivers turning several mills. But the town really took off when the C&O Canal and B&O Railroad came through in 1833-34. However, the town was virtually indefensible militarily because it sits in the bottom of a geographical bowl. (loc)

Miles had his headquarters here during his time at Harpers Ferry. He was brought back here after his mortal wounding. (kp)

Jackson's force, including the divisions of Lawton, J. R. Jones, and A. P. Hill, totaled just 11,000 men. As Jackson approached Harpers Ferry, he deployed his men on Schoolhouse Ridge to the west. (The walking trail, leaving from this parking lot, goes to the ridge and the Confederate position.) This ridge paralleled the Federal defense line on Bolivar Heights (to the east across the road which came to this stop). Jackson put Jones on his left (to the north), Lawton here in the center, and A. P. Hill on the southern portion of the ridge. With Jackson's deployment, he sealed Miles within Harpers Ferry from the west. When McLaws captured Maryland Heights and Walker arrived at 10:00 a.m. that morning, the Confederates surrounded Harpers Ferry.

Colonel Dixon Miles faced a conundrum. He had received several orders to hold Harpers Ferry at all costs. McClellan, however, had encouraged Gen. Henry Halleck to order the evacuation of Harpers Ferry, but Halleck refused—he believed McClellan's force moving west could relieve the garrison. Even with Miles's experience as a 38-year US Army veteran, he lacked dynamic leadership abilities. Instead of reading the situation for himself, he followed orders to the letter and remained in Harpers Ferry. Worse for his men, Miles also neglected to follow advice for defending his position. Instead of constricting his lines to Camp Hill and utilizing the Naval Battery for defense, he posted his men on Bolivar Heights. This stretched thin his force, and he did not have enough men to cover the entire heights. Miles did not believe the Confederates would be able to put artillery on Loudoun Heights, so he dedicated no forces there.

As mentioned before, communication between McLaws, Walker, and Jackson was difficult at best. Jackson wanted to give precise orders and directions about when the Confederate artillery should open up on the Federal position in and around Harpers Ferry. He attempted to communicate with McLaws and Walker by signal flags, but this devolved into an inexact science as Jackson dictated 150-word long messages. By September 14, the Confederates had placed their artillery on all the ridges surrounding Harpers Ferry. Even Loudoun Heights, which Miles believed could not be occupied by enemy artillery, contained five Confederate guns. As Capt. Edward Ripley of the 9th Vermont wrote, "we saw that the Rebels had spent a busy night on Loudoun Heights and were working like beavers on batteries in two places." Though Jackson had not yet given the order to open fire, Walker grew restless, and his guns opened around 2:00 p.m. Soon, all the Confederate guns bombarded Harpers Ferry and the helpless Federals. As Federal Lt. Henry Binney described it, "the cannonade is now terrific." The fight for Harpers Ferry began in earnest.

Remains of the bolts holding the pontoon bridges that were once here during the Civil War still remain—a small reminder of the past. (kp)

Exit the parking lot and turn right onto Bakerton Road. In 0.7 miles, turn left onto US Route 340. In 0.9 miles, at the next light, turn right onto Shoreline Drive. Continue straight onto Shoreline Drive to the Harpers Ferry National Historical Park fee booth. There is a fee to take the shuttle bus into Lower Town Harpers Ferry. Park in the Visitor Center lot and walk to the park visitor center; from here, ride the shuttle bus into the Lower Town.

GPS: N 39.316475, W 77.756992

From the Lower Town shuttle bus drop-off, proceed on foot down Shenandoah Street. In approximately 0.07 miles,

At the time of the battle, this hillside was clear of trees. This small viewshed gives you an idea of the perspective from here toward the Confederate position on Schoolhouse Ridge. It was near here that Jackson ordered his diversionary attack against the Federal line on September 14. (kp)

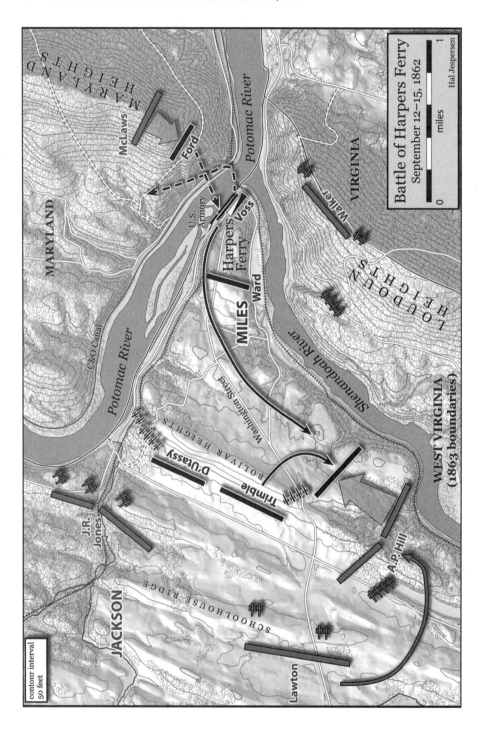

BATTLE OF HARPERS FERRY— As Confederates under Jackson and McLaws converged on Harpers Ferry from the east and west, the Federals under Miles made little preparation to defend the town or withdraw to safety. The terrain around Harpers Ferry made the town nearly indefensible.

take notice of two buildings on the right. The building labeled "Stipes Boarding House" served as Gen. A. P. Hill's headquarters following the surrender of Harpers Ferry; from here, he oversaw the paroling of the Federal prisoners. The next building on the right (today's National Park Service Information Center) was the headquarters of Col. Dixon Miles and also the building where he died on September 16, 1862. Continue walking along Shenandoah Street until it terminates. Turn right and follow the path underneath the railroad bridge. Continue straight to the row of benches. The Shenandoah River flows into the Potomac River here, and the area is known as The Point.

The Federal line at Bolivar Heights was a formidable position, especially from the west. Dozens of Federal artillery pieces lined these heights. The earthworks weren't constructed until 1864. For all of these defensive efforts, Bolivar was not defensible from Maryland or Loudoun heights, where enemy artillery could rain havoc from the east. (kp)

STOP 9: LOWER TOWN HARPERS FERRY

The noise of gunfire echoing from atop Maryland Heights into Harpers Ferry's Lower Town troubled Col. Benjamin "Grimes" Davis. Knowing that in this caged-in situation, his cavalry regiment would be useless to the Federal defense but his horses and cavalry equipment "of great value to the enemy if captured," Davis sought an escape. He took up his case with several officers, including Brig. Gen. Julius White. White, Davis, and the others rode into Harpers Ferry to speak with Miles at his headquarters (the Master Armorer's house, today's Information Center) about the situation.

Once Davis began the conversation, it quickly snowballed into a discussion about whether the entire garrison should attempt a breakout. Miles did not think it possible and rejected the proposal.

Today, the approximate wounding site of Col. Dixon Miles is a convenience store. Few travelers today know of the location's historical significance. (kp)

This sketch of Bolivar and Harpers Ferry dates from October 1862, when Federals moved back into Harpers Ferry after the battle of Antietam. The heights and few buildings that made up Bolivar are seen dotting the landscape. (loc)

Besides, his orders told him to hold Harpers Ferry, and he intended to do just that. Davis pressed his commander to at least let the cavalry try. Miles initially put down the idea but finally relented after an exchange of "sharp words."

The next night, September 14, the garrison's cavalry force, approximately 1,500 horsemen—in "the greatest secrecy"—lined up and down Shenandoah Street. Colonel Arno Voss commanded the force, which began crossing the pontoon bridge laid across the Potomac River at 8:00 p.m. Darkness and confusion confounded the crossing, but all the troopers reached Maryland within half an hour after the clandestine escape began.

Skirmishes with Confederate troops occasionally broke out along the march, including two in Sharpsburg. As the column continued making its way north toward Pennsylvania, it came across an enemy wagon train, bearing the reserve ordnance for James Longstreet's command. Incredibly, the Federal horsemen captured much of it in silence, taking 100 prisoners and reaping as many as 104 wagons.

Thirteen hours after the Union cavalry column vacated Harpers Ferry, it arrived in Greencastle, Pennsylvania, following a ride of fifty miles through the dark and behind enemy lines.

Known for his aggressive nature in battle, Maj. Gen. A. P. Hill showed glimpses of promise but continually clashed with his commanding general, Stonewall Jackson. Hill was placed under arrest by Jackson earlier in the campaign but was returned to command before the fighting at Harpers Ferry. (phcw)

Those wishing to move on immediately to Stop 10 should retrace their route to the shuttle bus drop-off and their cars. Those wishing to explore downtown Harpers Ferry as it relates to the September 1862 battle should leave the confluence of the Potomac and Shenandoah rivers and retrace their way along the path taken to get here. Cross Shenandoah Street and ascend the steps leading up the railroad embankment (there is a ramp farther ahead if one is required). Follow the dirt path past the obelisk marking the original location of John Brown's Fort, cross the now defunct railroad tracks, and proceed down the steps into the grounds of the old United States Armory at Harpers Ferry. Immediately turn right upon reaching the bottom of the steps and head for the boat ramp. This is the site of the pontoon bridge that carried the Federal cavalry across on the night of September 14. Return along the path to Shenandoah Street. Head in the direction of the shuttle bus lot. To the right, further up High Street, is a museum about Harpers Ferry in the Civil War (on the left side of High Street). Across the street from it is another museum exploring just the September 1862 battle of Harpers Ferry in greater detail.

Return to the Lower Town lot and take the shuttle back to your car parked at the Visitor Center. Upon exiting the Visitor Center parking lot, after passing the fee booth, turn right onto Shoreline Drive. Proceed 0.2 miles to the traffic light. Drive straight across US Route 340. In 0.2 miles, turn left on Whitman Avenue. Follow Whitman Avenue to the parking lot at the top of Bolivar Heights and park.

GPS: N 39.323802, W 77.761087

A. P. Hill supervised the parole of the Harpers Ferry garrison from the window of Cornelia Stipes's boardinghouse. Mrs. Stipes constantly had officers coming and going throughout four years of Civil War. (kp)

Brig. Gen. Maxcy Gregg was a lawyer and staunch secessionist from South Carolina before the war. Gregg was also a noted astronomer and owned his own observatory. Gregg rose in prestige during the war, and Hill placed his trust in him. He would be wounded at the battle of Antietam. (phcw)

A Congressman and lawyer before the Civil War, Brig. Gen. Lawrence O'Bryan Branch also held the distinction of finishing first in his class at Princeton in 1838. Branch started the war as a private and then rose to brigadier general in Hill's division. He was mortally wounded, supposedly by the same bullet that wounded Maxcy Gregg, during the later stages of the battle of Antietam. (phcw)

STOP 10: BOLIVAR HEIGHTS

Bolivar Heights, described by Confederates as "a position strong by nature," extended over two miles, running from the Potomac River to the Shenandoah River. Colonel Miles believed Bolivar Heights was his best chance for defense. Because Miles did not have enough men to cover Bolivar Height's entire length, many of his subordinates argued to abandon these heights and stage a more compact defense along Camp Hill, closer to Harpers Ferry. Furthermore, the Camp Hill defensive position had already proven strong that previous spring when, combined with the Naval Battery on Maryland Heights, a smaller Federal force successfully defended Harpers Ferry.

On the afternoon of September 14, Jackson ordered a Confederate feint toward this line. J. R. Jones's Confederates demonstrated along this portion of the line to draw the Federals' attention away from A. P. Hill's movement near the Murphy farm. The next morning, Miles realized his hopeless situation. Although he had sent messages out to McClellan, Miles was unsure if any were received; up to this point, he had heard nothing from the commanding general. McClellan, in fact, had ordered William Franklin and his VI Corps to move south from Crampton's Gap through Pleasant Valley to relieve the Harpers Ferry garrison, but Franklin, cautious and worried that McLaws's Confederates outnumbered his force, never made it.

Miles held a war council that decided to send out a flag of truce and to discuss surrender terms. As Miles made his way toward the front, an officer confronted him, protesting the surrender. Miles was quoted as saying, "They will blow us out of this place in half an hour." Soon after that prophetic confrontation, a shell exploded nearby and shattered Mile's left leg. The wound proved mortal, and Miles died in his headquarters the next day.

Take the walking loop trail around Bolivar Heights. A viewshed cut toward Schoolhouse Ridge gives a sense of the strength of the Federal position. There are also remains of Federal earthworks along the trail.

To visit the site of Miles's wounding, again driving, turn right out of the parking lot onto Whitman Avenue. Then turn left onto Alternate Route 340 (Washington Street). Travel 0.2 miles, locate the 7-11 convenience store on the right. In this general location Miles was wounded.

Turn around and continue on Washington Street until the stop light. Continue straight at the traffic light onto Shoreline Drive. Make the immediate right onto Campground Road (if you reach the visitor center parking lot, you have gone too far). Then take a left onto Murphy Road, follow this road to the Murphy House parking lot (Park Tour Stop 5). Several trails have signs that interpret the military action in this area.

GPS: N 39.312423, W 77.761145

STOP 11: MURPHY FARM

Many have criticized Miles's defense along the line of Bolivar Heights because he did not have enough men to cover the entire front. As Jackson lined up his divisions, he decided to use A. P. Hill's division as a flanking force to hit the Federal left on Bolivar Heights. Around 3:00 p.m. on September 14, Hill's men moved toward the Federal left near the Murphy farm. Hill ordered Gregg's and Branch's brigades to march along a small road beside the Shenandoah River. A large bluff hid the Confederates from the Federals along Bolivar Heights. The Federals did not have enough men to

Loudoun Heights is the second-tallest heights surrounding Harpers Ferry. Its rugged terrain led the Federals in Harpers Ferry to believe that it was not crucial to defend it. In 1861, Confederates under Stonewall Jackson built blockhouses on top of the heights to assist in defending the town below. Today, hiking trails, including the popular Appalachian Trail, lead up to Loudoun Heights. (kp)

Unionist Edmund Chambers and his family made their home at the Murphy farm at the start of the war, but Federal authorities forced the family from their home early in the war. After the war, the farm became "Brown Fort," the old armory engine house used by John Brown during his raid in 1859. The rebuilt fort sat on the property from 1895-1910. In 1906, W. E. B. DuBois and other leaders of the Niagara Movement, an organization of African-American leaders, made a pilgrimage to the restored Brown Fort. The Niagara Movement later grew into the National Association for the Advancement of Colored People (NAACP). The property was preserved in 2002. (kp)

guard this road but never thought the Confederates would be able to access the Union left by climbing the steep bluffs. That night Jackson sent Lee a message: "the advance which commenced this evening has been successful thus far, and I look to him for complete success tomorrow."

Early the next morning, the Federals woke up to a large Confederate force on their left near the Murphy farm. As Louis Hull of the 60th Ohio wrote, "A general feeling of depression observable in all the men. All seem to think that we will have to surrender or be cut to pieces." This movement forced Miles to reorganize his Bolivar Heights line and refuse his left flank to counter Hill's presence. At 6:00 a.m., 70 Confederate cannon from Loudoun Heights, Maryland Heights, and Schoolhouse Ridge opened up on the Federals. Federal artillery responded slowly to conserve ammunition. The Confederate attack plan called for the infantry to advance on the Federal lines after the Confederate artillery fire slackened. One Confederate wrote, "The bristling line of bayonets behind strong fortifications was a dangerous thing to approach and we knew that many of us would fall before we could hope to scale its ramparts and beat back its defenders."

As Hill's men began their advance around 7:30 a.m., white flags began to go up along the Federal line. Despite some confusion along the lines, the Confederates determined the Federal garrison was surrendering. Hill's action here at Murphy farm, combined with the artillery bombardment, convinced the Federals that further resistance was impossible.

With Miles lying mortally wounded in his headquarters, Brigadier General White oversaw the surrender of the garrison. The completion of the largest capitulation of Federal forces scored the Confederates 73 cannon, 13,000 small arms, 200 wagons, and more than 12,000 men. All totaled, Jackson lost only 39 killed and 247 wounded. Jackson sent a message to Lee about his victory, and with this news, Lee decided to remain in Sharpsburg and make a stand against the approaching Army of the Potomac. By 10:00 a.m., Jackson started his men on the road to Sharpsburg. Now, the Confederates were in a race against time to get to Sharpsburg before McClellan attacked Lee along the banks of Antietam creek.

Retrace the route back to Route 340 and turn left on Route 340 west. Travel 0.9 miles and turn right onto Route 27 (Bakerton Road). In 1.5 miles, make a sharp left to remain on Bakerton Road (now Route 28). Continue

Here along the banks of the Shenandoah and under the nose of the Federals near Murphy farm, A. P. Hill moved thousands of men and 20 cannon, then scaled heights to gain the flank of the Federal line. Imagine moving 2,000-pound cannon up these slopes. (kp)

A popular spot for Antietam buffs, Moler's Crossroads has signage that interprets A. P. Hill's famous march from Harpers Ferry to Sharpsburg. Modern research has looked at Hill's march more critically than the signage still suggests. (kp)

on Bakerton Road for 5 miles, to the Civil War Trails marker on the left in the parking area of the Bethesda United Methodist Church.

GPS: N 39.396069, W 77.764296

STOP 12: MOLER'S CROSSROADS

After the Federal garrison's surrender at Harpers Ferry on September 15, Jackson quickly moved his men (along with McLaws's and Walker's men) to join Lee at Sharpsburg. Jackson left A. P. Hill and his division behind to deal with the prisoners' parole and captured stores. Although Lee hoped that Hill would also arrive at Sharpsburg on the evening of September 16, Hill stayed in Harpers Ferry awaiting orders. Those orders arrived at 6:30 a.m. on the 17th, and by 8:00 a.m., Hill's men moved out toward Sharpsburg.

Unlike Jackson's command, which used the more direct and quicker Halltown Road to Shepherdstown and Boteler's Ford on the Potomac, Hill used what is now Bakerton Road. This added unnecessary distance (and time) to Hill's march, a total of twelve miles (although Hill's report states seventeen miles). The legend of Hill's supposedly quick march from Harpers Ferry to Sharpsburg and the subsequent saving of Lee's army has grown over the years. Recent research has shed more light on this episode. Yes, Hill opportunely arrived at the right time on the afternoon of September 17, but a twelve-mile march in eight hours was not quick by Civil War standards. Nevertheless, as Hill's force reached this point, it had shed nearly forty-percent of the men in his division. It was a hot day, and consequently, many men fell out. Even so, Hill's goal remained: Boteler's Ford on the Potomac and then on to Sharpsburg. He did not know how the battle was unfolding and rode ahead of his column to connect with Lee and learn where he should deploy his men.

Turn left onto Knott Road, then make the immediate right onto Route 31 (Engle Molers Road). Drive 1.6 miles to the intersection with Trough Road on the right. If you turn right here this road will take you to the location of Boteler's Ford (where the road ends). To continue with the rest of

Called Boteler's Ford or Packhorse Ford, the river crossing served the region since the early 1700s. Competing with the Blackford Ferry upriver near Shepherdstown and then a new covered bridge in 1850, the ford became more for local use than travelers. (loc)

the tour, continue on Engle Molers Road for 1.1 miles and make a right onto Route 230 (Shepherdstown Pike.). In 0.8 miles make a right onto South Princess Street. In 0.1 miles make a left onto German Street. Continue on German Street through downtown · Shepherdstown for three blocks (0.3 miles) and make a right onto Duke Street (Route 34). Continue for 4.2 miles (driving through Sharpsburg), the Antietam National Cemetery will be on the right, but the parking area for the cemetery will be on the left. After parking, walk either to the National Cemetery or the nearby community cemetery, Mountain View. From either location, look east. In this area Gen. Robert E. Lee witnessed much of the battle of Antietam.

GPS: N 39.460220, W 77.741819

STOP 13: ANTIETAM NATIONAL CEMETERY

In 1862, this hilltop provided excellent views for Lee to watch both his northern (left) and southern (right) flanks. Neither the National Cemetery nor the cemetery across the street existed at the time of the battle. From the far end of the National Cemetery, at the stone wall, visitors can look south to see the hilly terrain and ravines that encouraged Lee to make a stand here at Sharpsburg. Although many historians have criticized Lee for leaving his outnumbered force here with his back to the Potomac River, more recent scholarship shows that Lee knew exactly what he was doing on September

15 when he decided to defend the hills west of Antietam Creek.

Lee put Antietam Creek between him and McClellan, creating a natural barrier that the Federals would have to cross and re-cross if they wanted to reinforce either of their flanks. Lee followed this same strategy several times throughout the war. As an engineer, Lee knew how to read the land: the hills and ravines around Sharpsburg allowed for great defense, providing cover for his men to move, possibly even hiding large bodies of men. The Southern commander also knew the Northerner's reputation as a cautious commander. Possibly this terrain would cause McClellan to be guarded and make a mistake that Lee could exploit. Finally, Lee put all his "cards in" on this campaign. He truly felt if he could win a victory here in Maryland, the tide of the war could change. As he stood here, in this very spot, Lee decided to gamble and face McClellan in a battle that, from Lee's view, could determine the outcome of the entire war.

Established in 1867 for Union dead from the battle of Antietam, the cemetery is located on a dominant hill that Confederate leadership used to follow the flow of the battle. On the afternoon of the battle, portions of the Federal V Corps reached this spot but did not continue further, giving up a great opportunity to divide Lee's army. (kp)

Founded in 1883, Mountain View Cemetery is located on a hill that Lee used frequently before and during the battle to lay out his army and watch the opening action. Today the hill still provides a great view of the surrounding area. (kp)

Battle of South Mountain

CHAPTER FOUR

This route traces both armies' movements before, during, and after the September 14, 1862, battle of South Mountain. It follows both infantry and cavalry and will highlight notable locations associated with the battle.

"I have all the plans of the rebels, and will catch them in their own trap," George B. McClellan wired President Abraham Lincoln late on Saturday, September 13. Earlier that day, after various sources confirmed the veracity of Special Orders No. 191, McClellan moved his army west from Frederick, Maryland, and began executing his plan for September 14 "to cut the enemy in two & beat him in detail."

To do this, McClellan called on the bulk of his army—the I, II, IX, XII corps and Sykes's division—to strike Lee's "main body" at Boonsboro, a town on the western slope of South Mountain. McClellan ordered the three divisions under William Franklin's command to carry Crampton's Gap to the south. Following the successful passage of the mountain, Franklin's next objective was to liberate the Harpers Ferry garrison and disrupt the Confederate envelopment of that place. From there, Franklin could either turn north and help in the fight at Boonsboro or head west and cut off Lee's retreat to the Potomac River.

Meanwhile, the Federal army's immediate proximity and aggressive movements caught

Civil War correspondent George Alfred Townsend built the War orrespondents Memorial Arch on land he owned in Crampton's Gap. It honors Townsend's fellow journalists from the Civil War. (cm)

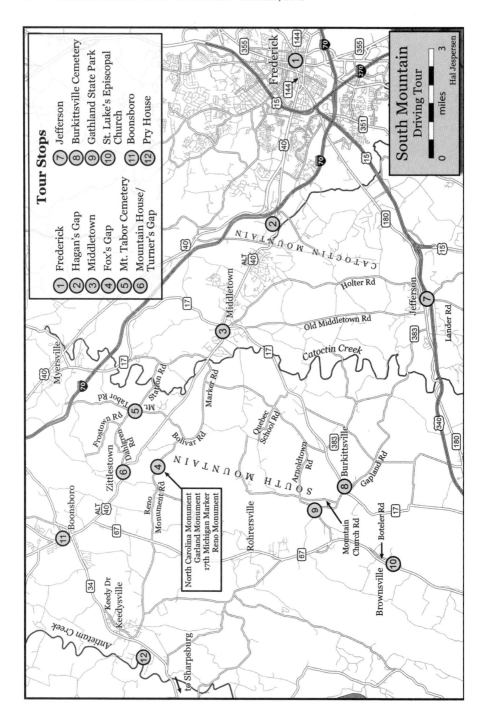

SOUTH MOUNTAIN DRIVING TOUR— This driving tour follows the Army of the Potomac as it approached Turner's, Fox's, and Crampton's gaps, which Confederates defended during the battle of South Mountain. After the Federal victory at South Mountain, the Army of Northern Virginia retreated to Sharpsburg.

Robert E. Lee off guard. His separated army was spread over twenty miles of Maryland and Virginia countryside and two major rivers divided it. Parts of the Army of the Potomac lay closer to Lee's Army of Northern Virginia than some of its far-flung brigades did to each other.

Incredibly, Lee's first thoughts turned to wrapping up the operations at Harpers Ferry and to protecting Maj. Gen. Lafayette McLaws's command in the valley, south and west of Crampton's Gap. He expected Crampton's Gap and Turner's Gap outside Boonsboro would be held by his army, while also impressing upon McLaws the importance of eliminating the Union force at Harpers Ferry immediately.

The tables turned suddenly on Lee's campaign, and both armies poised to engage in the first major battle north of the Potomac River.

Generals Jesse Reno and Ambrose Burnside made the Schley home their headquarters on the night of September 12. It still stands today at 423 East Patrick Street but is a private residence. Please respect the privacy of the residents. (kp)

The reactions of Frederick's citizens to the Army of the Potomac's arrival in their town proved to be a more widespread and joyous occasion than when the Army of Northern Virginia arrived days earlier. (loc)

The fate of Lee's invasion of the North —the fate of his army even—hung precariously in the balance.

Begin the tour of the Battle of South Mountain in front of the National Museum of Civil War Medicine, 48 East Patrick Street, Frederick, Maryland 21701.

GPS: N 39.413983, W 77.409270

STOP 1: FREDERICK

The fighting around Frederick began on September 12 at the Jug Bridge; then, it raged along Patrick Street from east to west before ending outside of Frederick.

Most of the Army of the Potomac marched along this road on its way to South Mountain. George B. McClellan rode along the main street, and the citizens enthusiastically welcomed him. "I was nearly overwhelmed & pulled to pieces," he informed his wife.

A Boston newspaper correspondent witnessed the pandemonium in the streets: "The people illuminated their houses, the Stars and Stripes were thrown to the breeze, patriotic songs were sung, handkerchiefs were waved, houses which had been closed for days were thrown open, and officers and men alike invited in, and the best the city could afford urged upon them, without money and without price." Worried his readers might not believe the scene, the writer reassured them, "this is no overdrawn picture; it will give the reader only a faint idea of the happiness imparted to the people of this place by the approach of a Union force . . . ."

For all the current excitement, the Union soldiers knew a fight was close at hand. Cannons' thunder echoed plainly in the distance.

Heros von Borcke, an officer on Jeb Stuart's staff, described Stuart's position at Hagan's Gap as "extremely favourable for defence." John Hagan's tavern, still standing today, stood in the midst of the September 13 fighting for Catoctin Mountain. (kp)

Proceed west on East Patrick Street, Route 144. In 2.9 miles, use the left turn lane to turn left onto Old National Pike, Alternate Route 40. Proceed 1.8 miles, and pull into the parking lot on the right next to the historic Hagan Tavern. Exit the vehicle and look back down US Alternate 40 toward the direction you just came from.

GPS: N 39.423477, W 77.493437

STOP 2: HAGAN'S GAP

After being expelled from Frederick on the 12th, Major General Stuart moved with Brig. Gen. Wade Hampton's brigade over Catoctin Mountain at this point into the Middletown Valley beyond. He left, here at Hagan's Gap, two guns and the Jeff Davis Legion under Lt. Col. William Martin to watch for Federal forces approaching from the east.

One brigade of Federal cavalry left Frederick the morning of September 13, and Martin's gunners soon greeted them. The blue-clad cavalry moved off the road and dodged for cover while two Union horse artillery batteries unlimbered before hurling their shells up the mountain. Dismounted Federal skirmishers ascended the mountain on either side of the road and found an enemy force in a superior

Brigade commander Wade Hampton commended William T. Martin for his and his soldiers' conduct at Hagan's Gap on September 13. The Jeff Davis Legion "fought with their accustomed gallantry," Hampton wrote, while Martin "conducted himself as a gallant and able officer." (loc)

Adam Koogle's house served as a headquarters for Jeb Stuart and the house served as a battlefield hospital, and the grounds became a battlefield in September 1862. A Louisiana Confederate wounded on the march stayed there, and A. C. Koogle, Adam's son, recovered from his Antietam wounds in his father's house. The younger Koogle served in a Maryland battery in the Army of the Potomac. (kp)

defensive position. The rest of Hampton's brigade arrived to add more substance to the resistance.

The infantry that was supposed to accompany Alfred Pleasonton's Federal cavalry had yet to reach the front several hours into the fight because of a wrong turn. Fearing Pleasonton could not take the pass unless he had infantry, army headquarters hurried Brig. Gen. Jacob Cox's entire division toward the fighting.

Simultaneously, the long column of Union troops rushing from Frederick and the successful Federal movement against one end of Hampton's line compelled Stuart to order the Rebel troopers off the ridge and into the Middletown Valley in the early afternoon. The Confederate stand here held back the Union tide for eight hours.

Pleasonton's troopers quickly remounted and began climbing into Hagan's Gap and over the side. "As we got to the top we pushed on faster and faster until we went down the further side at a gallop," said one Massachusetts man, involved in the chase. East of Middletown, Hampton turned part of his command, including some of his artillery, to face the pursuers. Federal horse artillery replied, and "after a sharp engagement of twenty minutes," Hampton's troopers pulled back again to their next position west of Middletown.

Turn right onto Alternate Route 40. Drive through Hagan's Gap (now called Braddock Gap) in Catoctin Mountain and observe the view of the Middletown Valley on your descent. About 1.9 miles from Hagan's Tavern is the area of Hampton's first stand east of Middletown; another 0.8 miles will bring you to the site of his second stand. Continue another 0.8 miles to the Civil War Trails signs on the left.

GPS: N 39.443897, W 77.547874

Laurence Baker's 1st North Carolina Cavalry lost eight men to wounds, with three others missing, during the fighting at Middletown. Baker, a West Point graduate, served throughout the war and suffered a serious arm wound at Brandy Station on August 1, 1863. (loc)

STOP 3: MIDDLETOWN

Just as the fighting east of Middletown neared its conclusion, a Yankee column swung around the town and attempted to cut off the inevitable Confederate retreat. Fortunately for those weary Rebel troopers, Col. Laurence Baker's 1st North Carolina Cavalry stood in the way. The North Carolinians, with the help of the mobile Confederate horse artillery, blocked the Federal threat long enough for the rest of Hampton's men to cross the covered bridge spanning Catoctin Creek at the west end of town.

With the creek between his cavalry and the enemy, Jeb Stuart ordered the bridge torched. Worried the fire would spread to his property, Adam Koogle, who owned the house and outbuildings abutting the span, implored Stuart not to burn the bridge; Stuart ordered it burned, anyway. "His offence was being a strong Union man," wrote one Northerner sympathizing with Koogle. The fire did, in fact, consume some of Koogle's buildings.

Koogle's house withstood the flames, but caught between the opposing artillery batteries, it sustained damage of a different sort. Koogle even lost one of his slaves to a shell.

Stuart now continued to pull his forces farther west and called for help. He reported to Maj. Gen. D. H. Hill, commanding a division of Confederates in Boonsboro, that the advancing enemy force consisted of a brigade of cavalry and two of infantry. Stuart thought Hill needed only one of his brigades to defend Turner's Gap in South Mountain. Once that brigade assumed its

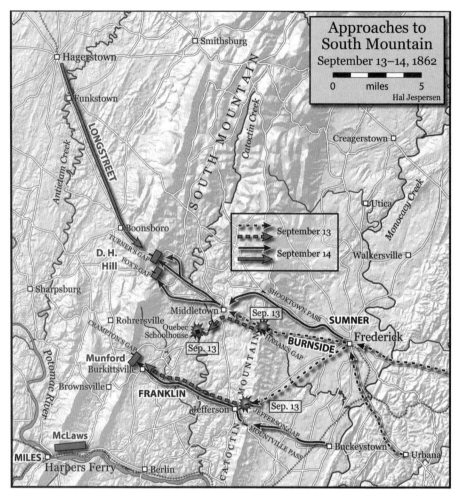

Approaches to South Mountain
September 13–14, 1862

0   miles   5

Hal Jespersen

September 13

September 14

APPROACHES TO SOUTH MOUNTAIN— Following the discovery of a lost copy of Special Orders No. 191, McClellan put his army in motion to attack the Confederate forces defending South Mountain the next day. Responding to the threat, Lee moved elements of James Longstreet's command from Hagerstown to buttress his defense atop South Mountain.

position in the gap, Stuart sent his troopers south to help protect Confederate forces engaged in securing Harpers Ferry.

On Sunday, September 14, most of the Army of the Potomac marched through Middletown on its way to the South Mountain passes. Here, "the inhabitants turned out en masse to welcome us and cheer us on our way to battle," remembered one Union soldier. "Never was a more cordial welcome given to troops than was given to us."

Despite the cheerful greeting, an uneasiness settled across the scene, with the distant rumbles of battle audible and the smoke on South Mountain easily visible from Middletown. "The people were more excited here as the cannon boomed loud and near, and bloodstained soldiers were coming in from the field of battle," lamented one Wisconsin man. On to South Mountain, they marched.

Continue west on Alternate Route 40. Drive 0.2 miles and take note of the private residence, 504 West Main Street. This home belonged to Jacob Rudy during the Civil War and is the place where Rutherford B. Hayes received medical treatment following his wounding at Fox's Gap. Continue traveling for 0.7 miles, when you will reach the Koogle house on your right. Just beyond that is Catoctin Creek and the site of the bridge Jeb Stuart ordered burned. Another 0.1 miles further, turn left onto Marker Road. You are now following the trace of the IX Corps to Fox's Gap. Travel on Marker Road, which turns into Bolivar Road and eventually becomes Reno Monument Road. After going 2.9 miles, notice the driveway to the left. In 1862, Eliakim Scammon's Federals used this road to reach the Confederate positions at Fox's Gap. Please respect private property. Continue up Reno Monument Road for 0.8 miles and turn left onto the paved road, followed immediately by a right turn into the gravel parking area.

GPS: N 39.470550, W 77.617641

STOP 4: FOX'S GAP

Exit the vehicle and, on foot, turn right out of the gravel parking lot onto the paved road. Walk 0.3 miles. Before

Alfred Waud sketched Union soldiers marching through Middletown on their way to the battle of South Mountain on September 14, 1862. The town later became a hospital for the wounded from both South Mountain and Antietam. (loc)

Today's Reno Monument Road follows the path of the wartime Old Sharpsburg Road, which continues straight in this image. Scammon's soldiers, the first Federals to attack Fox's Gap, followed the Loop Road to enter the gap, which is a driveway today but can be seen running towards the left of the photo. The oak tree under which Jesse Reno died stood near the intersection of Reno Monument and Fox Gap Roads until the late 20th century. (kp)

Jacob Cox did not have military experience prior to the start of the Civil War. By September 14, 1862, he commanded a division in the IX Corps, and he would tactically command the corps at Antietam three days later. (loc)

Mockingly called "Old Granny" by his soldiers, Eliakim Scammon served in many different theaters of the war. In 1864, Confederates captured him while asleep on a boat in West Virginia. (phcw)

the road bends to the right, take the left fork (a dirt trail) until you see the North Carolina Monument.

GPS: N 39.467421, W 77.618167

STOP 4A: NORTH CAROLINA MONUMENT

When the soldiers of Jacob Cox's Kanawha division stirred from their slumbers early on September 14, they did not expect to have a day of battle. Rather, they believed they were simply to accompany elements of Alfred Pleasonton's cavalry and occupy Turner's Gap in South Mountain, one mile north of Fox's Gap. An artillery duel along the National Road, which passed through Turner's Gap, showed Confederates strongly held Turner's Gap. Thus, the frontline Federal commanders deemed it more prudent to flank the enemy position at Turner's by occupying Fox's Gap to the south. Colonel Eliakim Scammon's Ohioans quickly headed off to their new destination.

Shortly before the Federals arrived in Fox's Gap, D. H. Hill sent Brig. Gen. Samuel Garland's North Carolina brigade to protect the south end of his line here. Hill told Garland to hold the gap "at all hazards." Garland's 1,100 men spread themselves over 1,300 yards to cover the position.

At 9:00 a.m., skirmishers from the 5th North Carolina and 23rd Ohio spotted each other—then began their violent sport. Soon, both regiments engaged in a deadly firefight. Lt. Col. Rutherford B. Hayes of the 23rd Ohio exhorted his soldiers: "Men of the Twenty-third, when I tell you to charge, you must charge." The Buckeyes did just that, forcing Garland's right flank back. A second Ohio advance kept up the pressure as Hayes went down with a shattered left arm.

In a hurry, Samuel Garland rode north to bring reinforcements to his crumbling right.

Take the dirt General Garland Trail back to the clearing along Reno Monument Road. Turn toward the left upon entering the clearing and find the small stone monument (it looks like a grave marker) to Samuel Garland.

GPS: N 39.470528, W 77.617333

STOP 4B: GARLAND MONUMENT

Virginian Samuel Garland's star was rising in the Army of Northern Virginia. The Virginia Military Institute (VMI) graduate had fought well on many other battlefields throughout the Eastern Theater. Now, with his back to the wall at Fox's Gap, Garland once again earned his peers' respect.

When the general arrived at the northern end of his line, Scammon's Ohioans began to press Garland's center and left. He observed the fight on his left, and despite pleas to remove himself from danger, he stayed. "I may as well be here as yourself," Garland told the 13th North Carolina's commander—just seconds before both were struck down. Garland's wound proved mortal, but his men continued to tenaciously hold on to their position, even fending off a Union battery at close range.

Dedicated in 2003, the North Carolina Monument sits along the line of Gen. Garland's defensive position at Fox's Gap. (kp)

North Carolina

In memory of the North Carolinians who fought at or near here September 14, 1862. The 1st, 2nd, 3rd, 4th, 5th, 6th, 12th, 13th, 14th, 15th, 20th, 23rd, 30th Infantry and Manly's and Reilly's Battery, 1st NC Artillery.

General D. H. Hill was in command of the Confederates with elements of Longstreet's Corps arriving in the afternoon. The fighting here at Fox's Gap saw one of the few instances of actual hand-to-hand combat of the war. The 13th NC was totally surrounded after the mortal wounding of Brig. Gen. Samuel Garland just a few yards from here. Two days after the battle, 58 Confederate dead were dumped down the well of Daniel Wise located NW. In 1874, they were reinterred in Hagerstown, MD.

Samuel Garland graduated from both the Virginia Military Institute and the University of Virginia prior to the outbreak of war. Division commander D. H. Hill lamented that Garland "had no superiors and few equals in the service." The small monument to him at Fox's Gap was placed on the battlefield in 1993. (b&l)

By 11:30 a.m., Jacob Cox had four Ohio regiments in position to strike, and they surged up the mountain, yelling and charging with the bayonet. The Carolinians began to break toward Turner's Gap, and the 13th North Carolina only narrowly escaped being surrounded. The Kanawha division held Fox's Gap after three hours of fierce fighting. Exhausted and aware of more nearby Confederates, Cox did not press his advantage. "Three hours of uphill marching and climbing had been followed by as long a period of bloody battle," Cox wrote. "It was time to rest."

Turn around to face Reno Monument Road. Walk toward the road. Across the road from the stone wall around the Reno Monument is a farm gate. Carefully cross Reno Monument Road, then find the marker titled "Stonewall Regiment." Stand with your back to the marker, facing the road.

GPS: N 39.470804, W 77.617196

STOP 4C: 17TH MICHIGAN MARKER

The early afternoon lull gave D. H. Hill the time he needed to rush more troops to the breakthrough and even provided him time to plan a counterattack to wrest control of the gap from the Federals. After deploying 4,000 men onto the Old Sharpsburg Road (modern Reno Monument Road) down the mountain's western slope, Hill left the field and entrusted Brig. Gen. Roswell Ripley with completing the task. But the deployment and terrain plagued the plan from the start. Only Brig. Gen. Thomas Drayton's brigade moved forward to fight the enemy in any serious fashion, striking the Federals south of the road.

Rutherford B. Hayes's wound at South Mountain was serious but not fatal—he lived to become the United States's 19th president. His friend William McKinley, another future president, also served in the 23rd Ohio during the Maryland Campaign. (phcw)

Union Brig. Gen. Orlando Willcox's IX Corps division soldiers met the attackers and drove them back. Drayton's men fell back to Reno Monument Road, facing south. The Confederate defenders soon came under attack from three sides, including the brand new 17th Michigan Infantry charging north of the road, bearing down on Drayton's left and rear. Unable to withstand such a tremendous fire, the Rebel line disintegrated. Drayton lost half of his men in the fight.

Shortly after the firing subsided, more troops came onto the field from both sides. The IX Corps commander, Jesse Reno, also rode forward to press his troops' success and secure his hold on the gap.

Carefully re-cross Reno Monument Road. Enter the stone enclosure and walk up to the Reno Monument. Standing with your back to the monument, face the road you just crossed.

GPS: N 39.470582, W 77.617024

Thomas Drayton fought against his brother Percival during the battle of Port Royal on November 7, 1861. Drayton's Brigade lost 206 men killed, 227 wounded, and 210 missing or captured in their fight at Fox's Gap. (phcw)

STOP 4D: RENO MONUMENT

Jesse Lee Reno, a martial figure of a career soldier, reached Fox's Gap about dusk that bloody Sunday. He arrived, consulted with his subordinates, and sent the 51st Pennsylvania into the field north of the Old Sharpsburg Road to sort out rumors of a nearby enemy force.

Reno remained mounted, carefully monitoring the Pennsylvanians. Suddenly, the flashes of Confederate muskets ignited the distant tree line. "There was at once a commotion" amongst Reno's party, "a dismounting and a catching of someone." Federal soldiers responded to the volley, and the luckless 51st Pennsylvania remained caught in the middle.

In the meantime, Jesse Reno, severely wounded by the Confederate volley, was brought down the mountain's eastern slope and laid under an oak tree. Reno did not live long after that, succumbing to his wound and his last words barely escaping his mouth: "Tell the boys that if I cannot be with them in body, I will be with them in spirit." The 39-year-old general was one of Fox's Gap's last casualties, and the first Federal corps commander killed in action during the Civil War.

All told, approximately 1,100 Southerners and nearly 900 Northerners fell in the 13-hour fight for the gap. Federal forces prevailed, gaining this important gateway over South Mountain by the end of September 14.

Orlando Willcox was captured at First Bull Run and not released from Confederate prisons until August 19, 1862. He commanded a division during the Maryland Campaign but had little time to get to know his subordinate and superior officers. (phcw)

A "renegade Virginian," as D. H. Hill called him, Wheeling, West Virginia, native Jesse Reno's loss was keenly felt by the IX Corps. At the battle of Antietam, when troops from the corps charged across the Lower (Burnside) Bridge, they yelled, "Remember Reno!" (loc)

Return to the car. Turn left out of the parking lot and carefully turn right onto Reno Monument Road. Travel 0.9 miles. Near the intersection of Reno Monument Road and Fox Gap Road on the left once stood the oak tree under which Jesse Reno died. Continue 0.3 miles on Reno Monument Road and turn left onto Bolivar Road. While driving on Bolivar Road, take note of the high ground on the right, which served as Federal artillery positions as well as Burnside and McClellan's command post during the battle of South Mountain. Travel to the stop sign, and carefully go straight through the intersection with Alternate Route 40 onto Mt. Tabor Road. Go 1 mile and turn right on Station Road (it comes up fast!). Immediately pull over on the left side of the road (you may wish to travel farther on Station Road and turn around first, pointing your car back toward the intersection). Exit the car, walk to the brick sign for Mt. Tabor Lutheran Cemetery, and face west toward South Mountain.

GPS: N 39.479615, W 77.588943

STOP 5: MT. TABOR CEMETERY

From his perch atop South Mountain, D. H. Hill watched more Union soldiers move toward his position. "The marching columns extended back as far as eye could see in the distance," he remembered. "It was a grand and glorious spectacle, and it was impossible to look at it without admiration. I had never seen so tremendous an army before, and I did not see one like it afterward." Not distracted for long, Hill called for the rest of his brigades to come to the mountaintop. Brigadier General Robert Rodes's Alabamians assumed a stretched-out position northeast of Turner's Gap. Newly-arrived soldiers from Maj. Gen. James Longstreet's command deployed closer to the gap.

Below the mountain, Maj. Gen. Ambrose Burnside ordered all of Maj. Gen. Joseph Hooker's I Corps, minus one brigade, north of the National Road to hit the Confederate left. Burnside envisioned Hooker's attack and Reno's at Fox's Gap enveloping both ends of Hill's defense of Turner's Gap.

"It looked like a task to storm," declared one blue coat. Hooker deployed his troops from his command post here at Mt. Tabor Church and sent them forward at 5:00 p.m. Men of the Pennsylvania Reserves dislodged Rodes's Southerners on Hooker's right and began pursuing them up the rugged slope. "All order and regularity were soon destroyed, and the battle partook of the nature of a free fight, every one going in 'on his own hook,' as it suited his fancy," recalled one Pennsylvanian.

The Reno Monument was one of the first monuments erected on a Maryland Campaign battlefield. It dates to 1889 and is supposed to mark the exact location of Reno's mortal wounding, but in reality, it stands about 200 yards from that spot. (kp)

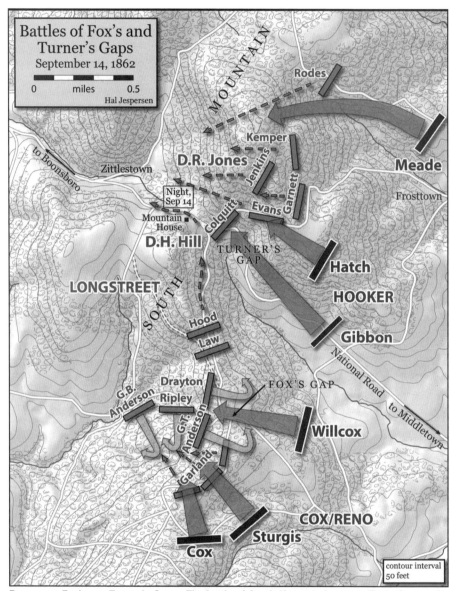

Battles of Fox's and Turner's Gaps—The battle of South Mountain began at Fox's Gap on the morning of September 14. Federal forces found early success there but could not follow up the victory. In the afternoon, Ambrose Burnside's entire wing—I and IX Corps—attacked D. H. Hill's and James Longstreet's troops defending the National Road on both their right and left flanks, forcing the Confederates to vacate the battlefield that night.

At the same time that Brig. Gen. George G. Meade's division stepped off its assault, John Hatch's Federals moved forward on the left of the line. Sweeping up the foothills of South Mountain, Hatch's line aimed for the newly-arrived elements of James Longstreet's command, fresh off a fifteen-mile march to reach the battlefield.

D. H. Hill witnessed Hatch's attack, which left a deep impression on his mind even years later: "Hatch's general and field officers were on horseback, his colors were all flying, and the alignment of his men seemed to be perfectly preserved" as they advanced. Confederate resistance initially held strong, but ultimately the Federals' onrush proved unstoppable: these Southern soldiers, like their counterparts to the north, likewise fell back toward Turner's Gap.

By sunset, nearly 600 Federals and over 900 Confederates had fallen in the fierce fighting north of Turner's Gap. Hooker's victorious troops failed to capture the gap itself, but his I Corps "had completely turned [Hill's] position" and "seized the commanding heights from which [Hooker] had driven the Confederates."

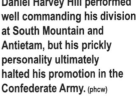

Daniel Harvey Hill performed well commanding his division at South Mountain and Antietam, but his prickly personality ultimately halted his promotion in the Confederate Army. (phcw)

There are two options to get to your next step. The first has better roads and terrain and follows the attack of the Black Hat (later known as the Iron) Brigade into Turner's Gap. The second weaves between Hatch's and Meade's divisions during their assaults. This route is over rougher roads and more uneven terrain; it should be taken with extreme caution.

Option One: If you have not already done so, turn your car around on Station Road to face the intersection of Station and Mt. Tabor Roads. Turn left onto Mt. Tabor Road. Travel 1 mile back to Alternate Route 40 and turn right onto the National Road. Drive 0.2 miles. Take note of the brick Henry Shoemaker house on the right (private property). Artifacts found in the house indicate its use by Gibbon's Wisconsin soldiers, likely as a field hospital during and after the battle. Drive on, considering that Gibbon's Black Hat Brigade advanced on either side of this road during its advance into Turner's Gap. Continue another 0.8 miles to the stone house on the left (private property). This home is another wartime structure, and the 2nd Wisconsin and 19th Indiana advanced behind it in their attack. In another 0.4 miles, at a bend in the road to the left, you will come to the approximate position of Colquitt's brigade. Continue up the mountain for 0.7 miles and turn left into the parking lot of the Old

Robert Rodes's Alabama Brigade lost 422 out of the 1,200 men it carried into action north of Turner's Gap. D. H. Hill wrote of Rodes's performance in his after-action report that he "handled his little brigade in a most admirable and gallant manner, fighting, for hours, vastly superior odds, and maintaining the key-points of the position until darkness rendered a further advance of the Yankees impossible." (phcw)

Though a critic of George B. McClellan, Joseph Hooker was promoted to command of the I Corps at the beginning of the campaign. Hooker's corps was in rough shape by September 1862, but McClellan believed Hooker would "soon bring them out of the kinks & . . . make them fight if anyone can." (loc)

South Mountain Inn.

Option Two: If you have not already done so, turn your car around on Station Road to face the intersection of Station and Mt. Tabor Roads. Turn right onto Mt. Tabor Road. Travel 0.1 miles, and veer left onto Frostown Road. Continue 0.5 miles to the intersection of Frostown and Dahlgren Roads. In the northwest corner of the intersection are remnants of a stone wall behind which Meade's division deployed for its attack. Continue straight along Dahlgren Road. In 0.5 miles, notice the O'Neil (foreground) and Haupt (background) homes, both wartime structures. Rodes's defensive line stretched through this area, and soldiers of the 3rd Alabama Infantry utilized the Haupt home in their defense. Carefully continue on Dahlgren Road for 0.6 miles. Along Dahlgren Road, Hatch's division attacked uphill to the left and Meade's division to the right. Notice the wartime stone walls on the right as you ascend the mountain. Continue on Dahlgren Road to reach an open plateau on the left after the road makes a sharp bend to the right. This is the area where Hatch's attack fell on the Confederate brigades of James Kemper and Richard Garnett. Continue driving on Dahlgren Road until the road descends to Alternate Route 40. Turn right onto Alternate Route 40. In 0.1 miles, turn left into the parking lot of the Old South Mountain Inn.

GPS: N 39.484397, W 77.620055

STOP 6: MOUNTAIN HOUSE/TURNER'S GAP

While the battle raged on both sides of Turner's Gap, Brig. Gen. Alfred Colquitt's brigade of Georgia and Alabama soldiers sat in a strong defensive position on either side of the National Pike, a half-mile to the east. Across the field from Colquitt, also astride the National Pike, stood Brig. Gen. John Gibbon's Black Hat brigade of Midwesterners, holding the Union center.

Ambrose Burnside placed Gibbon's men there to demonstrate directly against Turner's Gap as the fighting escalated to the north and south. The Wisconsinites and Indianans remained in place while the other attacks commenced, and they

During the advance against Turner's Gap, a bullet slammed into John Hatch's right leg, knocking him out of field command for the remainder of the war. In 1893, he received the Medal of Honor for his actions at South Mountain. (loc)

watched the battles up and down South Mountain with their front-row seats. Some observed the terrain, and one noted that Turner's Gap appeared "an ugly looking place to attack."

One member of Hooker's corps had a similar view of South Mountain from its base and remembered afterwards, "It looked like a task to storm." (kp)

Ugly or not, Gibbon's soldiers lunged forward into the Confederate rifles and cannon. The members of the Black Hat Brigade played a game of leap-frog amongst each other, in an effort to move forward amid the boulder-strewn, uphill climb in the face of Colquitt's fire.

Colquitt's Rebels proved a tough nut to crack. Utilizing the terrain to its advantage, the 28th Georgia gained the northern flank of Gibbon's assault and poured a plunging fire into the 7th Wisconsin. The 6th Wisconsin rushed in to drive back the enemy skirmishers but could do no more than that. The fighting escalated on both sides of the pike and continued unabated until dark. Colquitt wrote that the advances made upon his strong position "were kept back by the steady fire of our men." Indeed, they did just that. "Not an inch of ground was yielded," he reported.

The Confederate defenders suffered small losses—fewer than ten percent. Gibbon's Hoosiers and Badgers lost close to twenty-five percent of their strength, higher than any other Federal brigade engaged at South Mountain.

Alfred Colquitt graduated from Princeton University in 1844. He served as a postwar governor of Georgia and a United States senator. (loc)

After the fight subsided, Robert E. Lee consulted with Generals Hill and Longstreet. He had learned it would be unlikely to hold Turner's Gap much longer with Federals occupying key ground north and south of the gap. "The day has gone against us," Lee wrote one of his subordinates, "and this army will go by Sharpsburg and cross the [Potomac] River." For Lee, his excursion into Maryland was over.

Turn right out of the parking lot onto Alternate Route 40 and proceed back down South Mountain. In 2.6 miles, notice Marameade on the right, which served as George B. McClellan's headquarters during the battle of South Mountain. Drive another 2.1 miles and look for 504 West Main Street on the right. Here, Lt. Col. Rutherford B. Hayes initially recovered from his Fox's Gap wound. Continue 0.4 miles and turn right onto North Church Street, Route 17 South. Travel for 2.8 miles on what becomes the Burkittsville Road. A cavalry fight between Wade Hampton's troopers and Federals from the 8th Illinois and 3rd Indiana cavalries occurred here on September 13. Both sides bloodied each other in the inconclusive engagement. Continue straight on the Burkittsville Road. Turn left onto Route 383 South in 0.7 miles. In 1.3 miles, turn left to remain on Route 383 South. Travel 1.8 miles and turn left again to stay on MD-383 South. In 2.4 miles, turn left onto the Jefferson Pike, Route 180. Drive 0.8 miles before turning right at the light onto Lander Road. In 0.1 miles, turn left just beyond the gas station. Park and walk to the Civil War Trails sign. Note: This marker covers events related to the Gettysburg Campaign.

GPS: N 39.360353, W 77.531657

John Gibbon's brigade suffered 318 casualties while storming Turner's Gap. Its performance on September 14 earned them the nickname "Iron Brigade" in popular memory, though at least two other brigades claimed that same title in the Army of the Potomac. (loc)

STOP 7: JEFFERSON

Alfred Pleasonton sent his cavalry scouting in many directions on September 13. In addition to forwarding the bulk of his force toward Hagan's Gap, he also ordered the 6th Pennsylvania Lancers south from Frederick to reconnoiter the area around Jefferson.

Colonel Thomas Munford's depleted Virginia brigade patrolled this area. Two of his regiments manned Jefferson Gap, supported by a battery of horse artillery. Munford's guns kept the Lancers a safe distance away from the gap, and Union infantry marched to the troopers' support. After sighting Federal foot soldiers, Munford's cavalrymen withdrew toward Burkittsville at the foot of South Mountain.

On September 14, William Franklin's VI Corps crossed the Catoctin Mountain at Mountville Pass, one mile to the south, on its way to Crampton's Gap. "The ascent was long and very tedious," remembered one of Franklin's men. The climb loomed near the beginning of what proved to be more than a ten-mile march by the VI Corps to reach the Crampton's Gap battlefield and attempt to cut Lee's army in two.

Turn right out of the parking lot and proceed back to the light. Turn left onto Route 180. You will now be following the route that the Union VI Corps took to reach Crampton's Gap. Continue straight for 0.8 miles, and turn right onto Route 383, Broad Run Road. Travel 2.4 miles and continue straight onto Gapland Road. In 2.2 miles, at the four-way stop, is the Martin Shafer house and farm. William B. Franklin established his headquarters here during the Crampton's Gap fight, where he had a good view of the battlefield. In 0.6 miles, you will pass by Distillery Lane and the Harley house on the right.

The September 13 fight at Jefferson Pass resulted in minimal casualties. Federals pursued Munford's cavalrymen to Burkittsville before being turned back to Jefferson. (kp)

This spectacular view from Mountville Pass of the Middletown Valley between Catoctin Mountain and South Mountain greeted William Franklin's VI Corps soldiers before their descent into Jefferson on September 14. Crampton's Gap can be seen directly above the large barn in the foreground. (kp)

Harley, a civilian, accidentally provided the Federals with erroneous information about Confederate strength at Crampton's Gap. Travel 0.7 miles before turning right into the parking area for St. Paul's Lutheran Church. After parking, walk up the paved road to the cemetery entrance. Enter the cemetery and turn left where the road forks. Follow the path until another road intersects from the left. Stop there and turn left to face South Mountain.

GPS: N 39.394227, W 77.627777

STOP 8: BURKITTSVILLE CEMETERY

Henry Slocum's division led the assault against Crampton's Gap. By the end of the war, Slocum rose to command of the Army of Georgia during William T. Sherman's march through the Carolinas. (loc)

The Union VI Corps made the ten-plus mile march from east of Catoctin Mountain to Burkittsville in about six hours. The 96th Pennsylvania in the van of the corps reached Burkittsville about noon and immediately took fire from the enemy defenses near Crampton's Gap. Local civilians believed the Confederate defenses totaled over 4,000 soldiers (it was closer to one-quarter of that estimate) and informed the Federals of such. The false lead halted Franklin's Federals. Not wanting to stumble into something beyond what he bargained for, Franklin reconnoitered the Confederate positions while his troops spread out into their battle deployments.

While the VI Corps made its battle preparations, 800 Confederates under Thomas Munford's command readied themselves at the base of South Mountain. An additional 300 protected Brownsville Pass, about one mile south of Munford's command. The Confederate line west of Burkittsville consisted of dismounted Virginia cavalry and Georgia and Virginia infantrymen from Lt. Col. William Parham's brigade.

Franklin's subordinates did not complete their deployments until mid-afternoon, but by 4:00 p.m., a large formation stood north of Burkittsville ready to rush the Confederate line, which waited behind a stone wall along Mountain Church Road. Major General Henry Slocum's division formed a battle formation several lines deep. Once they advanced, the Confederate defenders poured shot and shell into the ranks. "The troops advanced steadily, every line in the entire column preserving its alignment with as much accuracy as could have been expected at a drill or review," Slocum reported.

The two opposing lines fired pounds of lead into one another, with the Southerners having the advantage of position. "Hot indeed was the fire which the rebs returned," remembered one gunpowder-grimed Yankee on the firing line.

The stalemate in front of Mountain Church Road raged unabated for over one hour. Eventually, "it became apparent to all that nothing but a united charge would dislodge the enemy and win the battle," said one Union brigade commander. With the sun sinking behind South Mountain, the vast wave of blue soldiers rushed forward on both sides of Burkittsville and scattered their stubborn adversaries, sending the Southerners scrambling up the mountainside with the Federals in pursuit.

Col. Joseph Jackson Bartlett was a lawyer in southern New York when the Civil War broke out. His superiors recommended him for a brigadier general's commission for his stellar performance in front of Crampton's Gap. Bartlett named the horse he rode on September 14, 1862, "Crampton" for the gap his men helped seize. (loc)

Return to the vehicle and exit the parking area the same way you entered, turning right onto Gapland Road/ West Main Street. In 0.2 miles, take note of the large stone David Arnold farm. William T. H. Brooks's Vermont Brigade traversed the farm in its attack on Crampton's Gap. Travel for another 0.2 miles and turn right onto Mountain Church Road. Continue along Mountain Church Road, site of the Confederate battle line. Along this battle line, attacking Union troops filled the fields to the right of this road during the engagement. Drive 0.7 miles. On the left once stood the Widow Tritt house; the left end of Munford's defensive line fought in

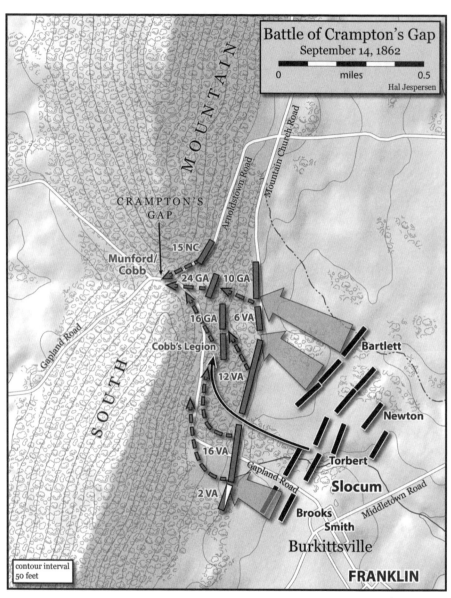

Battle of Crampton's Gap
September 14, 1862

0   miles   0.5

Hal Jespersen

MOUNTAIN

CRAMPTON'S GAP

Arnoldstown Road

Mountain Church Road

15 NC

Munford/Cobb

24 GA   10 GA

16 GA   6 VA

Cobb's Legion

Gapland Road

12 VA

Bartlett

Newton

16 VA

Torbert

Slocum

SOUTH

2 VA

Gapland Road

Middletown Road

Brooks

Smith

Burkittsville

contour interval 50 feet

FRANKLIN

BATTLE OF CRAMPTON'S GAP—A skeleton force of Confederate infantry and cavalry defended Crampton's Gap against William B. Franklin's VI Corps. The Federals won a sweeping success here, driving the Confederates completely off of South Mountain by nightfall on September 14.

this area. An intense, hand-to-hand fight occurred here shortly before the Confederate line broke. To your right stands the historic Henry Shafer farm, which Federal skirmishers occupied in the battle's early stages. Continue 0.4 miles and turn left on Arnoldtown Road. Travel 0.6 miles. Turn right into the parking area for Gathland State Park. Exit the vehicle and walk toward the large monument towering above the road. Carefully cross the road and stand underneath the archway, looking into Whipp's Ravine beneath this spot.

GPS: N 39.405766, W 77.639230
STOP 9: GATHLAND STATE PARK

When September 14 dawned, Brig. Gen. Howell Cobb had already positioned his brigade in Pleasant Valley, on the west side of South Mountain, behind this site. The buildup of Federal troops in Crampton's Gap prompted Lafayette McLaws to hurry as many troops as he could toward the pass. Cobb received his orders, which were to "hold the gap even if he lost his last man doing it."

The newly arrived brigade of Georgians and North Carolinians deployed halfway down South Mountain's eastern slope. Colonel Alfred Torbert's New Jersey men slammed into the Cobb Legion on the brigade's right, hitting the Georgians like a sledgehammer. The scrambled footrace up the summit began anew. Atop the mountain, Cobb worked like a madman to piece together some semblance of defense. The soldiers he gathered hunkered down behind the stone wall lining Padgett's field. Two artillery pieces aided the stand. Blasts of canister and the infantry firing only slowed the Federals rather than stopped them. Soon enough, the blue tide swept the Confederates from the field and firmly held the gap by dusk.

A setting sun gave McLaws a chance to find a solution to the problem Maj. Gen. William Franklin had just created for him. The VI Corps, worn out from its previous march and the intense fight up a mountainside, did not venture far from the mountaintop that night, finding whatever rest they could among the detritus of war. Franklin's men suffered over 500 losses; the routed Confederates lost double that. On September 14, McClellan's Army of the Potomac scored a victory, but the question remained: could the Federals "cut the enemy in two & beat him in detail"?

"The approach was through corn, over stubblefields and meadows, separated from each other by stone and zig-zag fences and spotted with thickets, stone piles, rocks, gullies, and quagmires," wrote one Federal soldier. He also deemed the enemy position along Mountain Church Road "one of the strongest and, naturally, most defensible positions held by either party during the war, and one of the most difficult to surmount." (kp)

Walk back to the vehicle and exit the parking lot, turning right onto Arnoldtown Road. At the intersection, carefully turn right onto Gapland Road. Travel 1 mile on Gapland Road. Turn left onto Route 67 South. Drive 1.1 miles and turn left onto Boteler Road. In 0.2 miles,

Howell Cobb's Brigade suffered heavily in its short but sharp fight at Crampton's Gap, losing 495 soldiers—nearly 40 percent of the brigade's strength. Before the war, Cobb served as a United States congressman, Speaker of the House, and Secretary of the Treasury before pledging allegiance to the Confederacy. His superior officers pinned much of the blame over what happened at Crampton's Gap on Cobb despite the difficult situation forced upon him when he arrived on the field. (loc)

you will pass on the left the old road that went over South Mountain at Brownsville Pass, the gap used by Lafayette McLaws's command to debouch into Pleasant Valley on September 11. Continue 0.7 miles and pull over on the right side of the road in front of St. Luke's Episcopal Church. Exit the vehicle and walk behind the church. Turn so your back is to the church.

GPS: N 39.373909, W 77.666575

STOP 10: ST. LUKE'S EPISCOPAL CHURCH

Federal successes at South Mountain and the stubborn Union garrison at Harpers Ferry isolated Lafayette McLaws's force in Pleasant Valley. "So here we are between two fires," one Southerner concluded. Working throughout the night of September 14, McLaws formed a defensive line across the valley floor near Brownsville facing Franklin's command. Much of his force squeezing Harpers Ferry loosened its grip on the garrison to bolster the line here. Robert E. Lee informed McLaws of the decision to exit Maryland, telling the boxed-in commander, "It is necessary for you to abandon your position tonight" and to join Lee's main body however possible. To McLaws, following the general's orders was impossible. "I had but to wait and watch the movements of the enemy," he wrote.

Meanwhile, sensing an opportunity on September 15, McClellan ordered Franklin "to open communication with Colonel Miles at Harper's Ferry, attacking and destroying such of the enemy as you may find in Pleasant Valley." Franklin balked. He found the enemy line in front of him and cautiously advanced toward it. The cacophony of cannon fire echoing up the valley from Harpers Ferry slowed, then ended altogether. Jackson and his Confederates finally swallowed up the Union garrison defending the town.

Franklin still posed a significant threat to McLaws, but he did not attack the Southerners. The nearly ensnared Confederates lived to fight another day, escaping through Harpers Ferry into Virginia before eventually rejoining Lee's main body at Sharpsburg.

Continue straight on Boteler Road. In 0.3 miles, turn right onto Route 67 North. After driving 3.2 miles, just past the intersection with Townsend Road, carefully look to the right; there, you will see the wartime John E. Crampton house (private property), William B. Franklin's post-Crampton's Gap headquarters. Travel another 6.2 miles through Pleasant Valley. Turn left onto Alternate Route 40. In 0.1 mile, cross a bridge. In this approximate area, Robert E. Lee established his field headquarters during the battle of South Mountain. Drive another 0.8 miles and find a place to park on Boonsboro's Main Street. Exit the vehicle and walk to the Civil War Trails signs at the intersection of Main Street and Shafer Park Drive.

GPS: N 39.509786, W 77.654048

Alfred Thomas Archimedes Torbert's men charged into Crampton's Gap with an axe to grind—especially the 4th New Jersey, which had almost entirely surrendered to the enemy at Gaines's Mill on June 27, 1862. "Remember the 27th of June!" yelled their colonel, William Hatch, as his New Jerseyans went into the fight. (loc)

STOP 11: BOONSBORO

Sensing a victory, McClellan ordered his various corps to push forward pickets early on September 15. They quickly discovered the vacant mountaintop and the Rebels' retreat, "and

Howell Cobb personally tried to stem the Confederate retreat by creating a last line of defense in Padgett's Field. Like other Confederate defenses that day, this one did not succeed. (kp)

Civil War correspondent George Alfred Townsend, who often wrote with the penname "Gath," memorialized 157 war correspondents with this 50-foot tall arch at the top of Crampton's Gap. The monument was completed in 1896. (kp)

an immediate pursuit was ordered." The foot race started to cut Lee off from the Potomac River.

General Israel Richardson's II Corps division led the pursuit. The pursuers saw the leftovers of the enemy withdrawal while passing down the mountain. "The road was strewn with their clothing & equipments & their wounded," said one. Confederate artillery fire greeted the Federals at the base of South Mountain. Richardson called forward the 5th New Hampshire to lead the movement, and the blue line lurched forward again, driving the enemy before them. When closer to the town, Richardson's infantry quickly moved off the road for Federal horsemen to continue the pursuit. One Confederate charge stymied the cavalrymen of the 8th Illinois, but only momentarily. The Illinoisans wheeled around and charged a second time, driving the enemy into the streets of Boonsboro.

In Boonsboro, several regiments of exhausted Virginia cavalry had dismounted to rest when the dash of the 8th Illinois Cavalry roused the Southerners. "Suddenly the order 'Mount!'

'Mount!' resounded down the street, and simultaneously a rapid fire of pistols and carbines was heard near at hand." A confused melee ensued, resulting in "a general stampede" of the Confederates toward Sharpsburg. Colonel W. H. F. "Rooney" Lee attempted to rally his men before a bullet struck his horse, bringing man and beast down together. The pursuit continued further toward Sharpsburg but ended well shy of Antietam Creek. Despite the brevity of the fight, losses from both sides proved severe, about 30 Union casualties and approximately 45 Confederate casualties.

Enter the vehicle and turn around to travel the opposite direction on Main Street from where you just came. In 0.3 miles from the intersection of Main Street and Shafer Park Drive, turn left onto Route 34 West, Potomac Street. This is the route of the Confederate retreat from South Mountain and the Federal pursuit. In 2.6 miles, turn left on Keedy Drive. This road is the historic trace of the Shepherdstown Pike. Travel 0.7 miles through the historic village of Keedysville, a wartime town. Turn right onto Coffman Farm Road. In 0.1 miles, on the

Lafayette McLaws experienced anxious times while at his headquarters at St. Luke's Episcopal Church. Following the Confederate defeat at Crampton's Gap, McLaws's division was wedged between two enemy forces—the Harpers Ferry garrison and Franklin's victorious Federals. McLaws established a defensive line in the vicinity of Brownsville facing the Federal VI Corps. It proved to be enough to prevent the destruction of his isolated force. (kp)

Edward Cross and his 5th New Hampshire Infantry spearheaded the Federal pursuit from Turner's Gap. Cross's fast-moving infantry earned the nickname "Richardson's foot cavalry" for their work on September 15. (loc)

Robert E. Lee's son "Rooney," commander of the 9th Virginia Cavalry, lost his horse in the fighting at Boonsboro and made a narrow escape back to friendly lines around Sharpsburg. (loc)

left, see the sign marking the headquarters site of George B. McClellan during the battle of Antietam. Continue straight on Coffman Farm Road. Turn left onto the Shepherdstown Pike, Route 34 West. Travel 1 mile and turn right into the driveway for the Pry house. Drive down the driveway and park in the lot to the right of the house. Exit the vehicle, walk in front of the house, and follow the paved path (it eventually becomes gravel) to the overlook behind the Pry house.

GPS: N 39.476028, W 77.714640

STOP 12: PRY HOUSE

The Army of the Potomac continued pushing its pursuit of the enemy army toward Sharpsburg. By the early afternoon of September 15, evidence began to indicate that the Confederate army was no longer retreating. Instead, they were making a stand behind Antietam Creek.

That morning McClellan had ordered his corps commanders to attack the enemy at once should they be found on the march. "If they were found in force and in position," he continued, "the corps were to be placed in position for attack, but no attack was to be made until I reached the front." McClellan reached the bluffs on the east side of the Antietam after 5:00 p.m. and did not like what he saw. His desire "to press" the enemy on the 15th vanished as he surveyed Lee's well-chosen position. "It was all a Rebel stronghold," said one Union observer. The roads of western Maryland also worked against the Union army, funneling the five corps pursuing from Turner's and Fox's Gaps onto one road, creating a massive back-up of Union troops between Antietam Creek and Boonsboro. McClellan had only two divisions ready for an attack. That and the late hour convinced him to delay the attack until the next day, and the evening of September 15th saw the logjammed Federal corps fanning out into their battle positions.

This concludes the Battle of South Mountain tour. To obtain a tour brochure to the Antietam battlefield, visit the Antietam National Battlefield Visitor Center at 5831 Dunker Church Road, Sharpsburg, Maryland 21782. If interested, the Return to Virginia tour begins there.

Philip and Elizabeth Pry suffered terribly because of the battle. Their house was Joseph Hooker's headquarters, George McClellan's command post, and the death place of Israel Richardson. The Pry's economic status plummeted after the battle, and they moved to Tennessee in 1874 to try and start a new life. (loc)

Both Robert E. Lee and George B. McClellan had a similar view in September 1862—Lee in the days before the battle and McClellan during the fighting. From near this vantage point, a Northern correspondent examined the Confederate position. It "was a broad table-land of forest and ravine, cover for troops everywhere, nowhere easy access for an enemy. . . . It was all a Rebel stronghold beyond." (kp)

Battle of Antietam
CHAPTER FIVE

The Antietam National Battlefield Visitor Center, 5831 Dunker Church Road, Sharpsburg, Maryland, is the best place to orient to the battlefield. The Return to Virginia tour also begins from there.

The dawn's fog on September 16 obscured the view of the opponents as they squared off across Antietam Creek. Once that fog burned off, George B. McClellan spent the morning and early afternoon examining the strong Confederate position lining Sharpsburg Heights. By 2:00 p.m., McClellan put his plan into motion. He ordered Maj. Gen. Joseph Hooker's 9,000 I Corps soldiers across the creek, planning this to be "the main attack upon the enemy's left." The remainder of the Army of the Potomac would maintain its positions and monitor the success or failure of Hooker's attacks and move accordingly. McClellan built his plan on flexibility.

Robert E. Lee's confidence grew as September 16 wore on. Two of Stonewall Jackson's three divisions and John Walker's division arrived from Harpers Ferry (A. P. Hill's remained there until the morning of

Burnside Bridge is one of the most iconic landmarks on any American battlefield. (kp)

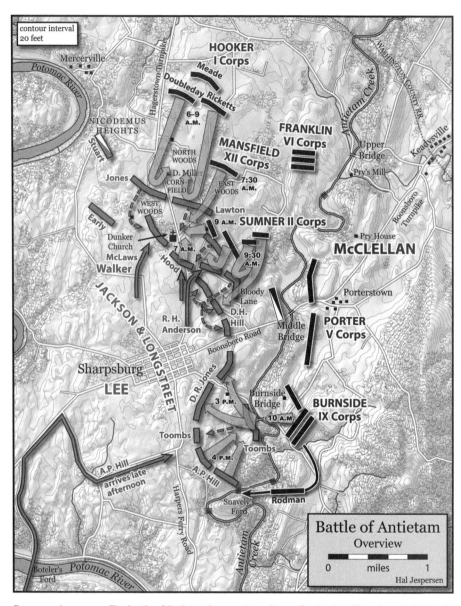

BATTLE OF ANTIETAM— The battle of Antietam began at sunrise on September 17 as Joseph Hooker's Federals advanced south towards Lee's left flank. Attacks by the Union I, II, and XII Corps made some lodgments in the Confederate line but failed to dislodge the Southerners from the field. A morning and afternoon attack on Lee's right led by Ambrose Burnside almost caved in Lee's line, but the last-minute arrival of A. P. Hill's division preserved the Confederate position at Sharpsburg.

September 17). Lafayette McLaws rushed his and Richard Anderson's divisions toward Sharpsburg, but they did not arrive until the early morning of September 17. Lee arranged his soldiers in their positions on the high ground around Sharpsburg, awaiting the movements of the Federal army.

Aside from desultory artillery dueling, the first contact between the two armies began toward dusk on September 16. A flair-up between George Meade's Pennsylvanians and Brig. Gen. John Bell Hood's Confederates in the East Woods proved inconclusive, ending only because of the onset of darkness. XII Corps reinforcements arrived overnight to support Hooker's movement.

As soon as the dawn's first light illuminated the landscape, Federals and Confederates in the East Woods continued the skirmishing begun the previous night. Hooker then sent two of his three divisions south from the North Woods toward his objective: the high ground opposite the Dunker Church. Confederate artillery crowning that high ground pounded the Union infantry. Confederate infantry positioned south of a 24-acre field of corn

The divisions of George Meade and James Ricketts used the Upper Bridge on the afternoon of September 16 as part of George B. McClellan's opening move of the battle of Antietam. Later that night and into the next morning, Joseph Mansfield's XII Corps likewise crossed here before taking up their prebattle positions. (kp)

owned by David Miller joined in the fight, and back-and-forth fighting engulfed the cornfield and surrounding woodlots. "There is a pandemonium of voices as well as a perfect roar of musketry and a storm of bullets. Shells are bursting among us, too, continually," one participant described of the early morning fight.

Joseph Hooker's first two divisions to move forward battered and bruised Jackson's Confederates (and received a similar bruising in the process). Forced to call on his last reserves, Jackson ordered the Deep South division of John Bell Hood into the fray. Screaming the rebel yell, Hood's infuriated soldiers crashed through Hooker's lines, sending the Federals back through Miller's cornfield. "It was here that I witnessed the most terrible clash of arms, by far, that has occurred during the war," reported Hood. Some of his men managed to temporarily pierce Hooker's reserve line under George

Stephen D. Lee had at least 15 guns posted on the Dunker Church plateau at the beginning of the battle of Antietam. His guns fired against Hooker's advancing Federal infantry, but enemy guns across Antietam Creek pounded Lee's position. The severe fire knocked 85 men of S. D. Lee's battalion out of action, and Lee called this place "artillery hell" for the rest of his life. (kp)

Meade on the cornfield's northern border, but ultimately, Meade's Pennsylvanians prevailed. Hood left 44% of his men lying on the field as the survivors quickly made their way to the Confederate rear. Despite Hood's repulse, Hooker's I Corps likewise suffered heavily (26% casualties) and could not continue the fight without reinforcements.

Fortunately for Hooker, just as his assault sputtered to a stop, around 7:30 a.m., Brig. Gen. Joseph Mansfield's 7,200 XII Corps soldiers started to appear on the field. Mansfield led his soldiers toward the cornfield and East Woods in tightly packed formations, making them ready-made targets for enemy artillery. Notably, more than half of his troops experienced their first combat just then (perhaps the reason for Mansfield's packing the volunteers tightly).

Mansfield found the battlefield situation unclear upon his arrival. Fixed on the idea that his XII Corps men should support Hooker's line, Mansfield rode for the front once he heard musketry erupt along his line. "Cease firing, they are our own men!" Mansfield shouted, before falling with a mortal wound.

Despite the loss of its commander, the XII Corps continued pushing on. It ran smack into Confederate forces shuttled north to the cornfield area in the early morning to support Jackson's line—three brigades of Daniel Harvey Hill's division. The seesaw fighting resumed while Brig. Gen. Alpheus Williams's division pitched into Hill's forces.

Soon, the Federal numbers began to tell, and the arrival of Brig. Gen. George Greene's division at the northeast corner of Miller's cornfield sent D. H. Hill's men—after a brief combat involving clubbed muskets and bayonets—streaming for the rear, with Greene's veterans in close pursuit. Ultimately,

George Meade's Pennsylvania Reserves stopped John Bell Hood's counterattack into Hooker's lines. Meade later praised his men, particularly Capt. Dunbar Ransom's artillery battery, for "repulsing the enemy" during "one of the critical periods of the morning." (loc)

John Bell Hood proved many times his worth to the Army of Northern Virginia. An able and aggressive commander, Hood's assault blunted Hooker's thrust but at a terrible cost—nearly half his division, 1,025 men, were casualties. (loc)

In the area around the cornfield, there were nearly 14,000 casualties combined from the two sides by the end of September 17. (kp)

Greene's soldiers pushed to the base of the Dunker Church plateau—Hooker's objective that morning—and cleared Confederate soldiers from the east side of the north-south Hagerstown Turnpike. But fatigue and an ammunition shortage prevented the breakthrough from being further exploited. Joseph Hooker also went down with a foot wound and had to be carried from the field.

In the two and a half hours of fighting, approximately 8,700 casualties fell in action in the area around the Cornfield. Joseph Hooker noted in the aftermath "every stalk of corn in the northern and greater part of the field was cut as closely as could have been done with a knife, and the slain lay in rows precisely as they had stood in their ranks a few moments before." The fighting on the northern end of the field was not over yet, though. Both army commanders rushed more men north of Sharpsburg, McClellan to follow up Hooker's and Mansfield's successes, and Lee to continue bolstering his left flank while seeking an opportunity to deal the Army of the Potomac a crippling blow.

Joseph Mansfield took command of the XII Corps on September 15, 1862. More than half the troops he commanded lacked any battlefield experience. Both theirs and their commander's novelty to battlefield situations showed. (nara)

Federal reinforcements came in the form of two divisions belonging to sixty-five-year-old Maj. Gen. Edwin Sumner's II Corps, more than 10,000 strong. When he reached the battlefield, Sumner could glean little information from anyone who might have the necessary facts and had to deduce what to do next. Eyeing the West Woods as important terrain for the Federals to hold, Sumner sent one of his divisions under Maj. Gen. John Sedgwick into that woodlot. Sedgwick's sledgehammer-like formation moved east-west into the woods while Brig. Gen. William French's trailing division headed south toward the remainder of D. H. Hill's Confederates, who waited in a nearby sunken farm lane.

Sumner personally led Sedgwick's soldiers across the blood-soaked ground strewn with the debris of war from the earlier fighting around the Cornfield. Sedgwick's lines

"Cease firing, they are our own men!" Mansfield yelled to soldiers of the 10th Maine Infantry shortly before falling mortally wounded. He died the next morning. This mortuary cannon marks the approximate location of Mansfield's mortal wounding. Five similar markers denote the locations of Antietam's five other generals killed or mortally wounded on September 17. (kp)

stretched in brigade front, three battle lines deep, heading west into the West Woods. As the Union troops entered the woodlot and barely broke through its western border, a scrambled force of Confederate infantry and artillery boldly stood in front of Sedgwick and briefly halted the massive formation.

Suddenly, the Federal soldiers noticed an increasing volume of fire west of them, and a more ominous roll of musketry resounded from the south. To support Jackson's battered legions, Lee, just an hour earlier, stripped Lafayette McLaws's division from its reserve position west of Sharpsburg and called on John Walker's division to hastily march from the southern end of the battlefield. These two arriving divisions converged at the right time and place, smashing Sedgwick's left flank and rolling up his line, sending blue-coated soldiers streaming in a panic from the West Woods back to their jump-off positions.

Alpheus Williams proved a reliable commander throughout the war, though his lack of a West Point degree may have held him back from deserved promotions. He handled the XII Corps ably after Mansfield's mortal wounding. (loc)

This Confederate success in the West Woods shattered the Federal Army's right flank but ultimately ran out of steam before it could mop up the Federals all the way back to the Antietam. Sedgwick's division lost approximately 40% casualties in roughly 20 minutes of action, significantly bloodied. While fighting in the Cornfield and West Woods sectors did not conclude with Sedgwick's repulse, the focus of the battle began to shift south, following French's division toward a worn-down farmer's lane, cutting through the landscape.

Near 9:30 a.m., while McLaws and Walker were pummeling Sumner and Sedgwick, French's troops ran into the Confederates of D. H. Hill, massed in a sunken farm lane— the left-center of Lee's Sharpsburg line. Three of Hill's brigades had made it into the cornfield that morning, but Brig. Gen. Robert Rodes's Alabamians and Brig. Gen. George Anderson's North Carolinians stayed back and now found themselves awaiting French's approach.

George Greene's division broke the back of the cornfield's Confederate defenders. Greene's men advanced all the way to the Dunker Church plateau and eventually beyond the church itself before being driven out in the early afternoon. (phcw)

For 70 percent of French's regiments, Antietam marked their first battle exposure. Like Sedgwick, French moved his soldiers toward the Confederate defenses three brigades deep. Max Weber's men led the way. With bayonets fixed, the Unionists reached the crest of a ridge fronting the

Photographs of the dead of the Antietam battlefield shocked the American public. The photos were, in many ways, the birth of photojournalism. These dead Confederates lay along the fences bordering the Hagerstown Pike. (loc)

Sunken Road position and walked into a sheet of flame belching forth from Rodes's and Anderson's rifles. "The entire front line, with few exceptions, went down in the consuming blast," recalled an Alabama colonel. One of Weber's regiments reportedly lost one-fourth of its men in that first volley. Shattered, Weber's now battle-hardened troops sought cover. French's second line passed over them, attempting to replicate the same tactics while Hill's Confederates fired on the advancing attackers. The third line, mostly made up of veterans, met the same fate, and the fight for the Sunken Road devolved into a slugfest.

Hoping to break the stalemate, Lee shoved another Confederate division—this one under Richard Anderson—into the fray to shore up Hill's line and push French's dogged soldiers off the high ground overlooking the Sunken Road. Unfortunately for the coordination of such an idea, Anderson went down with a wound early "and the consequent movements of his command were disjointed and without proper direction," wrote an early historian of the battle. Some of Richard Anderson's veterans pushed beyond the Sunken Road, but like Rodes's and George Anderson's men, failed to drive the Federals away from the road.

The Sunken Road fight continued unabated as the late morning wore on, and more Union soldiers pitched into the battle. Initially left behind on the east side of Antietam Creek while Sedgwick and French marched to the battlefield, Brig. Gen. Israel Richardson's II Corps division eventually came up in support of French's beleaguered ranks around 10:30 a.m.

Brigadier General Thomas Francis Meagher's Irish Brigade marched at the van of Richardson's reinforcements. After exchanging volleys at close quarters, Meagher attempted to charge en masse with his brigade against the stalwart Confederates. Like the previous three attacks, the Irish fell short of reaching the lane. By noon, though, the heavy fire and renewed pressure against the Southerners deteriorated their will to hold on much longer. Surges by pieces of the Irish Brigade and John Caldwell's newly committed brigade splintered the Sunken Road line and finally sent the Confederate defenders fleeing back toward Sharpsburg.

Aggressive Israel Richardson exploited the breakthrough, pushing his men west into the Piper cornfield and orchard. "Lee's army was ruined and the end of the Confederacy was in sight," thought one postwar Southern chronicler. However, as Richardson discovered, the end still remained elusive on

John Sedgwick's division suffered an astounding 2,228 casualties in the West Woods—40 percent of the division's strength—in less than 30 minutes of fighting. Sedgwick himself was wounded; later, he became the highest-ranking Federal general killed during the Civil War. (loc)

John Walker's division began September 17 south of Sharpsburg. Lee moved them north of town and, coupled with Lafayette McLaws's division, delivered a powerful blow to McClellan's right in the mid-morning. (phcw)

No regiment, Union or Confederate, suffered worse casualties than the 15th Massachusetts Infantry. By the end of the day, the regiment lost 318 men killed or wounded of the 606 it took into action—a 52 percent casualty rate. (kp)

this battlefield. Any Federal advance from the Sunken Road moved into the concave of a ring of Confederate cannon—53 in all— and Generals Longstreet and Hill led spirited rallies back toward the breakthrough. These measures convinced Richardson of the need for more artillery and men, and he pulled back to the Sunken Road to refit for one last drive. That never came. Confederate shrapnel struck Richardson, forcing him from the field.

Fighting around the Piper farm sagged after Richardson's wounding, and no further significant Federal assaults occurred in that area during the remainder of the day. Both army commanders instead turned most of their attention toward the south, where, simultaneously with the fight at the Piper farm, the Army of the Potomac secured another breakthrough.

Jacob Cox's IX Corps—under Ambrose Burnside's supervision—launched its first attack against the Confederate right between 9:00 and 10:00 a.m. By that point, only 2,400 Confederates under Maj. Gen. David R. Jones secured Lee's line south of Sharpsburg, with 400 directly defending the Lower Bridge crossing point while another 100 guarded the Antietam fords farther downstream.

William French's division consisted of more untested soldiers than veterans as it attacked the Sunken Road. In fact, the division had only been formed the day before the battle. (loc)

Burnside's and Cox's task was not easy. Not only did they have to fight just to get across Antietam Creek—a formidable obstacle itself on September 17—but they also had to carry the heights running south from Sharpsburg, an ascent of approximately 200 feet from their jump-off positions. Despite the disparity of numbers in the Union's favor, Jones's defensive post proved tough to crack.

The first IX Corps attack against the bridge did not go according to plan and badly fell apart. While the bridge attacks took place, Brig. Gen. Isaac Rodman's Federal division moved downstream, eyeing a place to cross the creek. This movement took longer than anticipated, so more Federals assaulted the bridge directly. A second attack likewise failed, but a third charge, aided by blue-coated infantry finding shallow crossing points both upstream and downstream of the Confederate defenders, forced the issue near 1:00 p.m.,

George Burgwyn Anderson commanded a brigade of North Carolinians during the Sunken Road fight. A Union bullet hit his foot and ankle and forced him from the field. The foot eventually had to be amputated, and Anderson never recovered from the surgery, making him one of Antietam's six generals killed or mortally wounded. (loc)

Richard Anderson's division did not attack in a coordinated fashion against the Federals storming the Sunken Road. Anderson fell wounded early in the fight. He later commanded a corps in the Army of Northern Virginia. (b&l)

"Faugh a Ballagh" shouted the Irishmen of Thomas Meagher's Irish Brigade as they charged towards the Confederates holding the Sunken Road. The Irish suffered heavily during the fight while Meagher, who fell from his horse in the midst of the battle, escaped—but had an accusation of drunkenness hanging over his head. (phcw)

three hours after the first attack had begun.

Before the IX Corps could surge west, however, its soldiers needed to replenish their ammunition boxes while thousands of men had to cross the narrow span (a crossing that had plagued them thus far) and deploy into their battle formations. By midafternoon, the Union line south and east of Sharpsburg stretched one mile in length with close to 10,000 troops in its ranks—soldiers from the IX and V Corps. Altogether, the Army of the Potomac's line west of Antietam Creek ran contiguously from south of the Lower Bridge to the North Woods.

Cox's soldiers lurched forward at 3:15 p.m. Orlando Willcox's division on the right of the line stepped off first and, assisted by their adjacent V Corps comrades, cleared Sharpsburg's Cemetery Hill of Confederates. Then they "rested partly in the town and partly on the hills." A lack of ammunition stopped any further forward movement.

Rodman's soldiers soon advanced toward the Harpers Ferry Road. The broken terrain of the Sherrick and Otto farms hampered their movements considerably, and gaps developed in the lines. Despite that, some of Rodman's command "in the full tide of success" came incredibly close to taking the high ground. David R. Jones's division began cracking while Robert E. Lee desperately sought to engage any available troops he could find—no matter how great or small—to aid his southern flank.

Suddenly, A. P. Hill's division arrived south of Sharpsburg. These men had just completed a tough march from Harpers Ferry but showed up at exactly the right time and place. Pitching into the fight in a downhill drive, Hill's soldiers smashed the left end of the Federal attack and began to roll up the blue line from south to north. The IX Corps soldiers obstinately opposed Hill's men but ultimately could not stop them. With the line's left flank shattered, the fought-out IX and V Corps soldiers pulled back toward their jump-off positions along Antietam Creek—back to the creek but not across it.

Hill's attack sputtered to an end around 5:30 p.m., shortly followed by oncoming darkness. The bloodiest single day in American history concluded, leaving approximately 23,000 men lying dead or wounded on the rolling hills, farms, fields, and roads of Sharpsburg.

To stop the Federal breakthrough at the Sunken Road, James Longstreet orchestrated Confederate counterattacks towards the position. He even ordered his staff to man a cannon while he personally directed the fire and held the horses. (loc)

Israel Richardson was the first Union general to arrive on the Antietam battlefield on September 15 and the last to leave it. He died in the Pry House from his Antietam wounds on November 3, 1862. (loc)

Return to Virginia
CHAPTER SIX

This tour concludes retracing the Maryland Campaign of September 1862. It follows the path of the Army of the Potomac's cavalry and infantry into Virginia in the fall of 1862 and ends in Warrenton, Virginia. The tour is approximately 110 miles in length.

The battle of Antietam wrecked the Army of the Potomac and the Army of Northern Virginia. Approximately 12,500 Federal soldiers fell on September 17 while Lee's commanders counted about 10,500 of their own casualties.

Despite the great bloodletting, neither army backed down from its positions along the Antietam on September 18. Both commanders explored options to renew the fight, but ultimately informal truces and flare-ups between skirmishers marked the day. Robert E. Lee began pulling his army away from Sharpsburg toward Virginia, although he saw this not as a retreat or end to the campaign. "When I withdrew from Sharpsburg into Virginia, it was my intention to recross the Potomac at Williamsport, and move upon Hagerstown . . . and endeavor to defeat the enemy at that point," Lee told his president. Limited Federal successes in Lee's rear at Shepherdstown and the presence of Union soldiers at Lee's intended re-entry point shut the door on his Maryland Campaign.

Welbourne, originally built in 1770 with additions, was the home of the Dulany family. Famous war-time visitors to the house were Jeb Stuart, John S. Mosby, and John Pelham. Welbourne was the scene of the Confederate cavalry's last stand on November 2, before moving westward to Upperville. (kp)

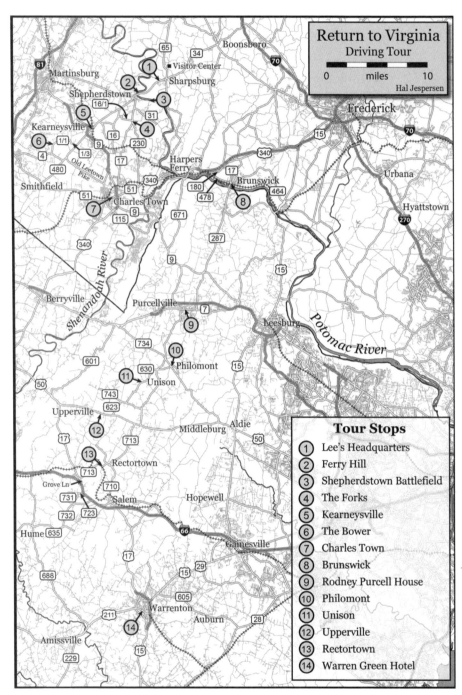

RETURN TO VIRGINIA DRIVING TOUR— This driving tour will take you from Sharpsburg, Maryland, to Warrenton, Virginia. You will follow elements of Confederate and Federal infantry, focusing on the cavalry battles in the Loudoun Valley that determined whether Lee's army could escape to safety.

The recent campaigns dating back to late June 1862 had drained the energy and manpower of the opposing armies. "The condition of our troops now demanded repose," wrote Lee while his counterpart George B. McClellan echoed, "I look upon the campaign as substantially ended & my present intention is to seize Harper's Ferry . . . . Then go to work to reorganize the army [and] ready [it] for another campaign . . . ."

Washington's patience with McClellan would only last so long, and prodded by Lincoln, the Army of the Potomac crossed into Virginia again in late October, inaugurating a new campaign in the war's Eastern Theater.

Jacob Grove's house served as first Robert E. Lee's and then Jeb Stuart's headquarters in Sharpsburg. Stonewall Jackson and James Longstreet visited the home, as well. (kp)

Start this tour at the Antietam National Battlefield Visitor Center, located at 5831 Dunker Church Road, Sharpsburg, Maryland 21782.

GPS: N 39.47407, W 77.74503

From the Antietam National Battlefield Visitor Center, turn left out of the parking lot and then left onto Route 65 (Sharpsburg Pike). Travel 0.9 miles and make a

Robert E. Lee's headquarters stood in a tent in an oak grove west of Sharpsburg. This area likewise served as a staging area for Confederate troops arriving from Harpers Ferry before being put into the battle line on the other side of town. (kp)

right onto Route 34 (Main Street). In 0.2 miles, Jacob Grove's large, brick house, which served as Robert E. Lee's first headquarters in Sharpsburg, appears on the left. Continue 0.6 miles to the site of Lee's headquarters on your right. The area is preserved as part of Antietam National Battlefield.

GPS: N 39.45520, W 77.76002

STOP 1: LEE'S HEADQUARTERS

One by one, Robert E. Lee's subordinate commanders gathered around the general's headquarters tent on September 17, reporting the situation in their sectors of the field. Then, Lee informed his generals there would be no withdrawal that night. Reinforce their lines and bring in the stragglers, Lee told them. They would not abandon the field.

George B. McClellan, likewise, did not give up the idea of a battle on September 18. During the night of the 17th, the commander resolved to have William Franklin's VI Corps renew the fighting on the battlefield's north end. McClellan also spent time orchestrating the arrival of additional Union reinforcements to aid in the next day's engagement.

The battlefield situation changed the next morning, though. Only some of the expected reinforcements arrived, and those that reached the battlefield did so by overnight marches, "fit for something," their commander assured. The big guns east of the Antietam that had plagued Confederate infantrymen and artillerymen on September 17 also awaited more ammunition—to the sum of 38 tons—that did not arrive from its circuitous trip to the front until late on September 18. McClellan delayed the attack until Friday, September 19, but by the time Franklin's soldiers rolled forward, Lee's Confederates had vanished. After unsuccessfully exploring options to steal the initiative of the campaign on September 18, Lee realized that only a drastic change might bring him victory in his Maryland campaign. That change involved moving his army back into Virginia, downstream from Shepherdstown, and then recrossing it upstream at Williamsport, thus bringing his men back into Maryland.

Lee's army began this difficult and ambitous maneuver under the cover of darkness on

Ferry Hill was the home of Stonewall Jackson staffer Henry Kyd Douglas. During the battle of Shepherdstown, Union cannon crowned the hill and engaged in a long-range artillery duel with Confederate guns guarding the river crossing. (loc)

September 18. Traffic jams and rain-soaked roads characterized the nighttime withdrawal. It was "some of the most tiresome and fatiguing work it was ever the lot of [the] army to do," recalled one soldier amidst the fits and starts. Miraculously, by early morning of September 19, the Potomac River lay between Lee's army and the Union army.

Continue on Main Street (previously Shepherdstown Pike) for 0.7 miles. Then make a left into a parking area for two Civil War Trails signs that cover the events that took place here at the Grove farm after the battle of Antietam. Continue for 1.6 miles and make a right into the entrance for Ferry Hill (part of the C&O Canal National Historical Park). The parking area will be on your left, and Ferry Hill is next to the parking area.

William Nelson Pendleton graduated from West Point in 1830 but spent most of the three decades prior to the Civil War as a clergyman. Many of the men and officers in the Army of Northern Virginia lost faith in Pendleton by September 1862, yet he retained his position as the army's chief of artillery throughout the war. (loc)

GPS: N 39.43802, W 77.79782

STOP 2: FERRY HILL

Federal cavalry reacted quickly to the Army of Northern Virginia's disappearing act. Following the visible trail of a maneuvering army toward the Potomac River, the horsemen arrived here in mid-morning only to come under fire from Lee's rearguard, one mile downstream from here at Boteler's Ford. Artillery chief William Nelson Pendleton directed the 44 guns and 600 infantrymen guarding the passage across the river. Union horse artillery posted here reacted to Pendleton's thumping artillery, but the Confederate gunners frustrated the blue-coated artillerymen's designs. Fitz John Porter's V Corps arrived at the front, shuttling more guns to silence Pendleton and feeding the infantry to the mostly dry C&O Canal, on the north side of the ford, to pick off the enemy gunners. McClellan's orders to his commanders along the river suggested against crossing "unless you see a splendid opportunity to inflict great damage upon the enemy without loss to yourself." Though opportunities lacked earlier in the day, by dusk Porter's tactics ensured abundant opportunities to damage the enemy.

Pendleton hoped to hold out until dark, but

Following the success of his limited September 19 operation against the Confederate rearguard at Shepherdstown, V Corps commander Fitz John Porter ordered a heavier reconnaissance the next day, which resulted in the battle of Shepherdstown. It was the last battle in which Porter commanded troops before being cashiered from the army. (loc)

his gunners alerted him about low ammunition. His slackening fire prompted Porter to try to "inflict great damage" upon Lee's rearguard. A few hundred Federals plunged into the Potomac—some hitting the ford directly, others missing—and prompted a hasty Confederate retreat. Casualties in this quick raid proved minimal, but it had great implications on Lee's plan. Fleeing south from the ford, Pendleton stumbled through the darkness to find his commanding general. He told Lee that he had lost all of the artillery guns. "All?" Lee stammered. Pendleton replied affirmatively. With such a significant loss and unknown enemy force in his rear, Lee slammed on his army's brakes, bringing the movement on Williamsport to a temporary halt. A large portion of Lee's soldiers trudged back to Boteler's Ford to drive the Federals back to their side of the Potomac.

Boteler's Ford was used multiple times by both armies during the Civil War, including during the Maryland Campaign, Gettysburg Campaign, and Jubal Early's foray into Maryland in 1864. (kp)

Turn right onto Route 34 (Shepherdstown Pike) and travel for 0.8 miles (crossing the Potomac River into West Virginia). Make a left onto German Street and travel through downtown Shepherdstown for 0.6 miles;

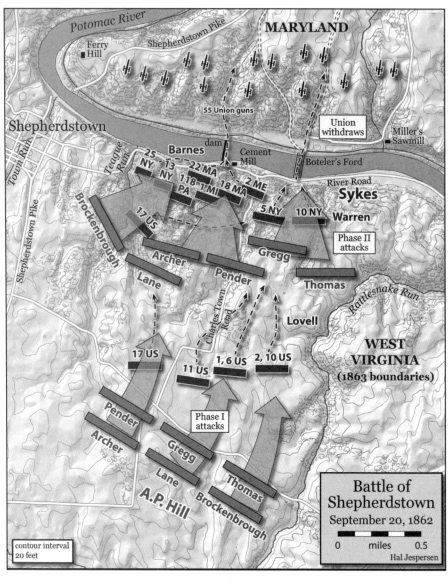

Battle of Shepherdstown
September 20, 1862

contour interval
20 feet

0   miles   0.5

Hal Jespersen

BATTLE OF SHEPHERSTOWN—Union forces crossed the Potomac River into Virginia on September 20 after scattering the Confederate rearguard defending Boteler's Ford the previous night. A. P. Hill's division met the Federals and drove them back across the Potomac while under heavy fire from the Federal guns posted on the bluffs north of the river.

German Street will become River Road. Continue on River Road for 1.1 miles (the Potomac River will be on the left). Interpretive markers for the battle of Shepherdstown stand at the intersection of River Road and Trough Road. Boteler's Ford across the Potomac River is in this general vicinity. Be careful as there is limited space to pull your car over.

GPS: N 39.42790, W 77.77862

STOP 3: SHEPHERDSTOWN BATTLEFIELD

Emboldened by his success the previous evening, Fitz John Porter proposed another river crossing on September 20. This two-pronged reconnaissance would determine the location and the intention of the Confederate Army toward Shepherdstown and Charlestown. An early Union raiding party secured a multitude of abandoned enemy supplies, including a battle flag and four pieces of artillery.

The two Union brigades, numbering 2,800 soldiers, crossed after 7:00 a.m., led by Charles Lovell's US Regulars. Lovell's men moved south toward Charlestown while James Barnes's volunteer brigade headed west for Shepherdstown. About one mile south of the ford, Lovell's men ran into the vanguard of A. P. Hill's division, sent back to the ford by Robert E. Lee to clear the enemy from his rear. Hill's men drove Lovell back to the river.

Division commander Gen. George Sykes, supervising the Federal foray south of the Potomac, recognized the area south of Boteler's Ford as a poor place for battle, with a river and tall bluff at his soldiers' backs. He conveyed this to Porter, who agreed it was time to end the reconnaissance. Sykes ordered Barnes to get his brigade onto the bluffs to support Lovell, and Gouverneur Warren's brigade also aided Lovell's fallback. Additionally, 55 Union guns north of the ford pummeled Hill's men in the advance. Lovell's and Warren's soldiers made it back to Maryland relatively unscathed, but Barnes's men, particularly the green 118th Pennsylvania, ran into trouble.

James Barnes had extricated much of his brigade from A. P. Hill's encircling division, but a mix-up in orders—or intentions—left the 118th Pennsylvania alone on the bluffs. Hill's overwhelming numbers began to tell; his brigades, lapping around the flanks of the Pennsylvanians, finally forced a rout. The Keystone State infantry scrambled down the steep bluffs and through ravines to make its way back to the river. Those who made it that far had to run a gauntlet of lead across a cement milldam to return to safety.

George Sykes commanded the division composed of all of the United States Regular infantry in the eastern theater. Nicknamed "Tardy George," a moniker dating back to his West Point days and not necessarily reflective of his battlefield performance, Sykes rose to corps command before Gettysburg but in 1864 was transferred to the Trans-Mississippi for the rest of the war. (loc)

The battle of Shepherdstown was James Barnes's first battle in command of a brigade. His brigade suffered 321 total casualties on September 20—269 of which came from the 118th Pennsylvania. (nara)

The 118th Pennsylvania Infantry mustered into service on August 31, 1862. It suffered a terrible baptism of fire at Shepherdstown, where commander casualties, confusion, the soldiers green nature, and defective rifles plagued them and forced horrendous casualties among the ranks. (hw)

Federal gunners prevented any Confederate pursuit, and the Maryland Campaign ended along the shores of the Potomac.

McClellan's pursuit cost the army dearly—363 casualties in the two-day fight at Shepherdstown, with nearly 75% of them from the 118th Pennsylvania. Confederate losses amounted to 285. However, the pursuit, and McClellan's sealing off of Lee's reentry point at Williamsport, worked. Realizing his army's physical condition and inability to respond effectively to his orders, Lee called off the campaign. The Army of Northern Virginia settled in the lower Shenandoah Valley while the Army of the Potomac encamped along the north bank of the Potomac. Both armies resupplied, refilled their ranks, and nursed their wounds until the next fight.

This stop concludes the sites related to the Maryland Campaign. The rest of this tour recounts the time between the end of the Maryland Campaign and George B. McClellan's removal from command.

Turn right onto Trough Road and travel for 1.6 miles. The initial actions of the battle of Shepherdstown took place to the right of this road. Turn right onto Route 31 (Engle Molers Road), travel for 1.1 miles and make a left onto Route 230 (Shepherdstown Pike). Continue for 1.3 miles to where Route 230 branches off to the left and Route 17 (Flowing Springs Road) branches off to the right. This area is known as "The Forks." Although the space to pull over is limited, a small monument in the intersection is publicly accessible.

GPS: N 39.399624, W 77.809628

STOP 4: THE FORKS

October arrived with action. Both armies launched raids into each other's territory, hoping to disrupt the recuperation period or gain much needed information. Both sides carefully concealed and guarded information, and ports of enemy strength and location proved difficult to discern.

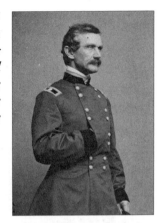

Andrew Humphreys, one of the most profane men in the Army of the Potomac, led his men in a reconnaissance-in-force towards Kearneysville on October 16. Humphreys later rose to the position of chief of staff of the Army of the Potomac. (loc)

In response to a report received at Federal headquarters on October 15 that the Army of Northern Virginia had withdrawn from Winchester, McClellan ordered a reconnaissance into Virginia to ascertain the truth. Brigadier General Andrew Humphreys led a force of 6,000 infantry, 500 cavalry, and six guns south from Shepherdstown and worked in concert with Winfield Scott Hancock, leading a similarly numbered mixed force from Harpers Ferry toward Charles Town.

Humphreys's contingent advanced to Kearneysville on October 16, driving elements of Jeb Stuart's cavalry "from position to position" to get there. After accomplishing his objective (as will be seen at the next stop), Humphreys fell back toward the Potomac the next day. Near the Forks, Lovell's brigade served as the column's rearguard. Confederate cavalry charged, attempting to cut off the Federal column from the river. Lovell's Regulars loosed a volley into the horsemen, "emptying many saddles . . . ." Federal cavalry and artillery arrived to support Lovell, and the entire column safely made its way to Maryland.

Return to the intersection and make a left (west) onto Gardner's Lane. Travel 1.3 miles and take a left to remain on Gardner's Lane. Continue for 0.5 miles and make a left onto Route 16 (Ridge Road). Travel for 0.8 miles and make a right onto Edgewood School Road. Continue for 1.3 miles and make a right onto Warm Springs Road. After 0.3 miles, make a left onto Route 480 (Kearneysville Pike). Travel 1.1 miles into the town of Kearneysville, turn into the bank parking lot after passing the intersection with Charles Town Road.

GPS: N 39.387528, W 77.885804

These small obelisks, like Marker No. 6, were erected beginning in 1910 by the Jefferson County Camp of the United Confederate Veterans. Their purpose is to mark the site of 25 battles and skirmishes throughout Jefferson County during the war. (kp)

STOP 5: KEARNEYSVILLE

Humphreys's reconnaissance force reached Kearneysville by the night of October 16. It passed through the railroad town, heading south the next morning, and encountered stiff enemy resistance. Determined to make it farther into Virginia's interior than Kearneysville, Humphreys put the full weight of his force onto the road, driving the Southern line back to Leetown. To confirm the enemy position, 25 horsemen continued the next few miles to Smithfield and found the objects of their search. "[T]he objects of the reconnaissance had been accomplished," Humphreys reported before falling back toward the Forks and the river. Lee's army had not vacated its position near Winchester.

Turn left out of the parking lot onto Leetown Road. Travel 2.2 miles and make a right onto Strider Road. In 0.9 miles make a left onto Bowers Road. Travel 1.9 miles (straight through the intersection with Payne's Ford Road) to a gravel pull off on the right side of the road. To the right will be Opequon Creek. After reading this segment on the Bower, continue on Bowers Road; immediately to the left is the Bower. The brick house is a private residence so please respect the property owner's privacy.

GPS: N 39.367064, W 77.957687

STOP 6: THE BOWER

The Dandridge family home—the Bower—became Jeb Stuart's headquarters in the wake of Antietam. Stuart safely monitored enemy movements from this central location, but he also filled his time here with merriment. In a home full of young, attractive women, dance, song, and revelry became the norm, punctuated by occasional work to be done.

Jeb Stuart used the Bower as his headquarters following the Maryland Campaign. One eyewitness to this event wrote that Stuart's camp here "was the envy of all the commands." While here, Stuart purchased a horse, Lucy Long, for Robert E. Lee. (dd)

Winfield Scott Hancock succeeded to command Israel Richardson's division after the latter's mortal wounding at Antietam. Hancock later became one of the Army of the Potomac's best corps commanders. He ran on the Democratic Party presidential ticket in 1880 but lost to fellow Civil War veteran James Garfield. (loc)

Charles Town served an important role many times during the Civil War, from the site of John Brown's execution in 1859 to the Shenandoah Valley Campaign of 1864. A meeting here on September 17, 1864, between Ulysses S. Grant and Philip Sheridan precipitated Sheridan's successful campaign. (loc)

Following some discussion, Lee gave his cavalryman instructions on October 8 to prepare for another of his now famous raids behind enemy lines. Lee ordered Stuart to head for Chambersburg, Pennsylvania. Ruin infrastructure, gather intelligence, and capture horses and political hostages, instructed Lee.

Stuart prepared 1,800 horse soldiers and four cannon for the expedition. The cavalrymen dashed across the Potomac River on the morning of October 10, reaching their goal by nightfall and taking horses as they went. Chambersburg fell to Stuart's force, who took whatever military supplies they could and destroyed what they could not.

Now sitting in the rear of the Army of the Potomac, Stuart veered away from retracing his path back into Virginia and instead took a route in a circular fashion around the enemy army. It seemed a near-run feat at times. Stuart's horsemen rode 80 miles non-stop to make it to the Potomac River near Leesburg by October 12. The cavalry commander's only worry was a brief scare at the river crossing. The raiding party did not lose a man during the nearly 130-mile ride, captured 1,200 horses, and damaged enemy infrastructure. Union cavalry proved unable to stop Stuart's ride. Returning to the Bower on October 13, Stuart and his Southern cavaliers celebrated their accomplishments with a grand ball two days later. One participant noted, ". . . the ladies of the neighbourhood [sic] were brought to the festivity in vehicles captured in the enemy's country, drawn by fat Pennsylvania horses. Stuart was, of course, the hero of the occasion, and received many a pretty compliment from fair lips."

Continue on Bowers Road for 1 mile and make a left onto Route 4 (Sulphur Springs Road). Travel 1.3 miles and take a left onto Leetown Road. In 0.4 miles, make

a right onto Old Leetown Pike and travel for 4.6 miles. Take a right onto North Mildred Street and continue for 1.6 miles. At the traffic circle, take the third exit to stay on Mildred Street. Take a left onto Route 51 (East Washington Street). Travel 0.6 miles and make a left into the bank parking lot that is before the Charles Town Racetrack.

GPS: N 39.293293, W 77.847902

The Army of the Potomac crossed here at Berlin between October 26 and November 2, 1862. It was the last campaign on Virginia soil for George B. McClellan, whose relationship with the Lincoln Administration continued to sour between the battle of Antietam and his crossing into Virginia six weeks later. (loc)

STOP 7: CHARLES TOWN

Winfield Hancock's reconnoitering force left Harpers Ferry at daylight on October 16, working alongside Humphreys's command to discover the enemy's whereabouts. First contact came about halfway between Harpers Ferry and Charles Town. Hancock's force drove back the Confederate pickets until encountering a more obstinate defense: four Confederate guns. Then, massed Federal artillery—perhaps as many as 16 guns—pounded the Southern artillerymen. The combined weight of the raining iron and Federal infantry forced the Confederate defenders away from Charles Town, which the Federals quickly occupied.

One eyewitness to the Federal crossing of the Potomac River described it as "a perfect picture. The still running water, with the long line of troops crossing it and then winding away into the country, was beautiful beyond my powers of description." (loc)

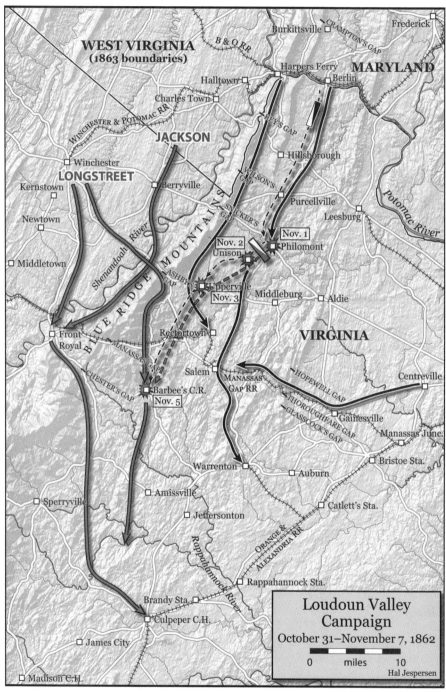

LOUDOUN VALLEY CAMPAIGN— After the fighting at Antietam ended, Lincoln expected McClellan to quickly follow Lee's army into Virginia. Lincoln himself visited McClellan and urged him to move his army to capitalize on his accomplishments in Maryland. Eventually, McClellan began to advance south. The cavalry fighting in the Loudoun Valley determined McClellan's fate as the commander of the Army of the Potomac.

General McClellan himself rode to Charles Town, arriving shortly after the town's occupation. Hancock, like Humphreys, achieved the objective of his mission and so returned his troops to Harpers Ferry the next day. McClellan returned to his headquarters in Maryland, too, plotting his next advancing route into Virginia.

Take a left out of the parking lot onto Route 51 (East Washington Street). This will become Route 340. Remain on Route 340 for 10.5 miles (passing Harpers Ferry) and take a right onto Route 180 (Knoxville Road). Then take your next right onto Route 478 (Knoxville Road). Continue on Knoxville Road for 2.2 miles (becoming Potomac Street upon entering Brunswick, Maryland). Make a right onto South Maryland Avenue, then a left into the parking lot for the Brunswick MARC station. A Civil War Trails marker, facing the train tracks, is located on the southern end of the parking lot. Though the marker focuses on the events here during the Gettysburg Campaign, it does mention the events of October 1862.

GPS: N 39.31224, W 77.62781

STOP 8: BRUNSWICK

Following weeks of back-and-forth traffic along the telegraph lines between Washington and McClellan's headquarters, McClellan assented to advancing south through the Loudoun Valley, as Lincoln outlined to him. The advantages of such a move could put the Army of the Potomac "on the inside track" between Lee's army in the Shenandoah Valley and Richmond.

The Army of the Potomac started crossing its namesake river here at Berlin (modern-day Brunswick) on October 26, but the crossing took several days. Thousands of men rumbled across the wooden pontoon bridge laid over the river. As each successive mass of soldiers reached the Old Dominion, "lusty cheers spontaneously broke from twenty thousand throats, awoke responsive echoes from the Virginia hills, and announced that the third campaign was commenced."

McClellan's objective through all of this focused on the area around Culpeper Court House. Hopefully, if he reached it soon enough, his army would be squarely between Lee's soldiers bottled up in the Shenandoah Valley and their capital city. "A race now ensues between Lee's Army, West of the Blue Ridge, and McClellan's Army, East of it, both marching south," described Gen. Abner Doubleday. Who would reach his objective first depended upon speed and the actions that would unfold in the Loudoun Valley.

Return to South Maryland Avenue and make a right. Travel 0.2 miles to the traffic circle and take the fourth exit off the traffic circle to Route 17 south (Petersville Road). Route 17 south will cross the Potomac River into Virginia and become Route 287 (Berlin Turnpike). After crossing the bridge, continue 12.7 miles and make a right onto Route 7 Business (East Main Street). Stay on East Main Street for 1.1 miles. The Rodney Purcell house will be on the right (second house after the intersection with North Hatcher Street). There is limited parking here, and the home is a private residence. Please respect the owner's privacy.

Today the historic Purcell House, which has been altered over the years, is privately owned. Few people traveling by the house today realize its Civil War history and its role in the founding of the town of Purcellville. (kp)

GPS: N 39.13678, W 77.71344

With Lee's infantry posted in the Shenandoah Valley at Martinsburg and Winchester, Stuart's cavalry was tasked with moving into the Loudoun Valley to shield the Confederate retreat up the Shenandoah Valley and to slow down the Federal southern advance. Stuart's men crossed the Blue Ridge Mountains at Snicker's Gap and guarded the gap until all Confederate infantry cleared the pass. (loc)

STOP 9: PURCELLVILLE - RODNEY PURCELL HOUSE

Named after local merchant Rodney Purcell, who operated a store here and lived next door, the town of Purcellville sat on the road from Leesburg to Winchester. In October 1862, this village lay in the path of the Army of the Potomac as it moved southward through Loudoun County. By Sunday, November 2, McClellan, along with Maj. Gen. Burnside, took up quarters here at the Purcell house. McClellan knew the pressure that was on him; Lincoln expected a speedy movement south to block the Confederate route eastward. McClellan received several conflicting reports of Confederate whereabouts. Some reports put Confederate infantry entering Loudoun County via Snicker's Gap, and others had the Confederates moving southeastward via Front Royal. McClellan relied heavily on his cavalry commander, Brig. Gen. Alfred Pleasonton, and his horsemen to scout ahead of the infantry, securing intelligence and assisting to slow down any Confederate infantry moving out of the Shenandoah Valley toward Culpeper. As stated before, whichever force got to Culpeper first determined control of the Confederate supply lines and communication with the Southern capital, Richmond.

At this time, Lee and his commanders received reports of the Federal movement southward through the Loudoun Valley. The Army of Northern Virginia was divided, with Stonewall Jackson's wing near Martinsburg, tearing up the

Brig. Gen. Alfred Pleasonton was either loved or hated by his colleagues. He was known for his over-the-top self-promotion and inability to gather accurate information. He was new to division command that fall and was recovering from a wound suffered in his right ear by the explosion of an artillery shell at the battle of Antietam. (loc)

Col. Williams Wickham served as the commander of the 4th Virginia Cavalry during the campaign, but due to an injury to Fitzhugh Lee, Wickham became the commander of the brigade. A Unionist before the war from Richmond, Wickham voted against secession but went with his native state when Virginia passed secession. (phcw)

B&O Railroad, and Longstreet's wing encamped near Winchester. Lee moved quickly once he realized McClellan's movement southward. Lee ordered Longstreet to Front Royal and Chester Gap where he could cross the Blue Ridge Mountains and march south on the Richmond Road to Culpeper. He recalled Jackson to Winchester, directing him to follow Longstreet. In this race the Confederates had the disadvantage of a longer route than the Federals. Lee ordered Jeb Stuart and his cavalry to the Loudoun Valley to slow down the Federal advance and buy some time for Lee. With extra time, he could get his infantry in front of McClellan and consolidate Confederates in Culpeper.

Head west on Main Street for 0.5 miles and make a left onto Route 690 (32nd Street). Take Route 690 south for 5.5 miles and make a left onto Route 734 (Snickersville Turnpike). Drive 0.9 miles, to find the Civil War Trails marker on the left in front of the store building. Park on the other side of the store.

GPS: N 39.05649, W 77.74043

Today the village of Philomont consists of a country store, a fire station, and a few homes. Local preservationists and conservationists fought in the 1990's to preserve the historic character of the Snickersville Turnpike (Route 734). (rgmhaa)

STOP 10: PHILOMONT

Major General Stuart arrived in the Loudoun Valley on October 30 via Snicker's Gap. He brought with him a 1,000-man cavalry brigade under the command of Col. Williams Wickham. Major John Pelham and his six-gun artillery battalion also joined Stuart. Before confronting Pleasonton's cavalry, pushing southward ahead of the Army of the Potomac, Stuart first had to oppose a smaller Federal force coming westward from Fairfax County under Brig. Gen George Bayard. These men moved out to support the advance of the Army of the Potomac. Stuart surprised elements of Bayard's cavalry at Mountville. This aggressive action forced Bayard to retreat to Fairfax Courthouse and out of the Loudoun Valley campaign.

When one drives Jeb Stuart Road from Philomont to Unison, one is transformed back to the 19th century. Here the road fords North Fork, just as it did in 1862. (kp)

Moving southward from Purcellville, Pleasonton commanded nearly 1,200 Federal cavalry. He also had at his disposal nearby infantry, which he could call upon if needed. His objective was to secure the route south for the main Federal infantry and to block any Confederate advance from the west. On November 1, Pleasonton arrived here in Philomont, eyeing Upperville (13 miles to the southwest). At Upperville, Pleasonton could watch the important mountain gaps the Confederates might use to move eastward from the Shenandoah Valley.

Around noon, the Federals began to move out from Philomont toward Unison (on present day Jeb Stuart Road). The road crossed a local stream, the North Fork; the easily passable ford here with heights on the opposite side created an ideal place for the Confederates to oppose the crossing. As the Federals rode down to the stream, shots rang out. From the firepower, the Federals knew this was more than just a partisan force or enemy scouts; more probably, the Federals faced an organized body. Quickly, the Federals pushed the 3rd Virginia Cavalry back across the North Fork and up to the heights beyond. Here, Pelham arrived with his artillery, forcing the Federals to stop. Similar to his famous action a few months later at Fredericksburg, Pelham ordered his guns from knoll to knoll, constantly moving, so the

The Loudoun Valley is home to many preserved landscapes and historic roads. Local groups like the Unison Preservation Society and the Mosby Heritage Area Association have worked hard to preserve the area. Visitors today can drive roads that have changed little since 1862. Use caution, as many roads are narrow and prone to flooding. (ro)

The Mosby Heritage Area Association educates and advocates for the preservation of the incredibly extant historical landscape in Northern Virginia. It was founded in 1995.

Federals could not determine his location. The fighting along the North Fork seesawed back and forth until, eventually that night, the Confederates moved back to the next defensible position near Unison.

Pleasonton now realized the difficulty of the route to Upperville. That night he ordered up infantry from Col. William Hoffman's brigade of the I Corps as well as additional artillery. McClellan expected his cavalry to arrive the next day as far south as Piedmont Station (modern day Delaplane). Stuart's objective focused on slowing the Federals, not to defeat or stop it. That night as Stuart camped near Unison, lead elements of the Confederate infantry under Longstreet crossed the Shenandoah River at Front Royal. Jackson's wing stretched from Millwood north to Snicker's Gap. Culpeper and safety lurked forty-five miles away, nearly a three-day march. Stuart needed to continue to delay the Federals—bloody days lay ahead in the Loudoun Valley.

From the Philomont Store parking lot, make a right onto Route 630 (Jeb Stuart Road). This stretch of road is one of the best preserved historic roads in the region. The road will actually ford the North Fork as it did in 1862 (if you do not wish to ford the creek in your vehicle, use the GPS coordinates below to direct you to the next stop). At the intersection of Jeb Stuart Road and St.

The Unison Methodist Church was built in 1829 to replace an earlier log structure. Federal soldiers left their marks behind on the walls inside of the church. The building was used as a hospital after the fighting around Unison. (rgmhaa)

Louis Road, continue straight onto Unison Road. Travel 2.3 miles, and the Civil War Trails marker will be on the left in front of the Unison Methodist Church.

GPS: N 39.03437, W 77.79336

STOP 11: UNISON

Now that Stuart realized he faced Federal cavalry and infantry, he knew that to slow the Federals' advance south with his small force, he would need to use the terrain and mobile tactics. As the sun rose on Sunday morning November 2, the bells here at the Unison Methodist Church rang, calling people to service. North of here, along Dog Branch, Stuart's skirmishers again challenged a Federal creek crossing. As the Confederates fell back, they moved south and formed up on the ridge that ran through the center of Unison. Pelham moved his six guns north of Unison Road, behind modern-day Bloomfield Road. As Pelham fired over the village into the oncoming Federal cavalry, residents scattered for cover. South of Unison Road, Federal cavalry dismounted and began moving toward Unison. North of Unison Road, Hoffman's infantry brigade began to move out of the Dog Branch valley toward the village. Now, Stuart's 900 cavalry and six cannons faced nearly 2,500 Federal infantry and cavalry with twelve cannons.

Maj. John Pelham was a rising star in the Army of Northern Virginia in 1862. Known for his good looks, Pelham excelled in the art of horse artillery. He was able to use his quick maneuvering tactics to delay the Federals in their pursuit of Stuart's cavalry in the Loudoun Valley. (loc)

Stuart's aide, Heros von Borcke, wrote about the town between two dueling artillery batteries: "furious flames, leaping from one another to these great masses of combustible material, and the dense volumes of smoke rolled from them, added to the terror and confusion of the scene." At 1:00 p.m., after delaying the Union men half a day, Stuart received information about another defensible position to his rear, near the Quaker Meeting House, and ordered his men to withdraw from Unison. He continued to use his delaying tactics at the Quaker Meeting House, then Beaverdam Creek, and finally at the day's close, near modern-day Welbourne Road and Quaker Lane. Stuart used mobile tactics of dismounted cavalry while Major Pelham employed his famous tactic: setting up his artillery, firing several shots until the enemy gained the range to his position, then mounting and moving his artillery to a different nearby ridge. This constant moving slowed down the Federal advance. By 6:00 p.m., the Federal advance under Pleasonton had covered only five miles in ten hours. It was a bloody day; nearly 100 total casualties fell on November 2. Stuart behaved admirably; he had slowed the entire Army of the Potomac's movement south. McClellan's plan disintegrated into shambles as the Confederates

Today, Welbourne is preserved as a bed and breakfast and a working farm. (rgmhaa)

west of the mountain continued their fast-paced march south and over the mountains to Culpeper. Stuart's next defensible position focused on the hills around Upperville and the important Ashby Gap in the Blue Ridge Mountains.

Turn left out of the church parking lot onto Unison Road and travel for 1.2 miles; then make a right to remain on Route 630 (Quaker Lane). Travel for 1.7 miles and take a right onto Route 743 (Welbourne Road). Travel for 0.5 miles and take a left onto Route 623 (Willisville Road). Continue on Route 623 for 1.6 miles before taking a right onto Route 50 West (John S. Mosby Highway). Travel 1.2 miles and make a left into a small park. Two Civil War Trails markers stand along the circle driveway.

GPS: N 38.99054, W 77.87222

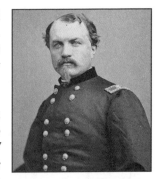

Newly promoted to brigadier general on September 26—though not confirmed until March 1863—William Averell was a West Point graduate who had served in several capacities in the Federal army in Virginia. By the time of the fighting in the Loudoun Valley, Averell had just returned from a serious case of malaria. (loc)

STOP 12: UPPERVILLE

As the sun rose on Monday, November 3, Stuart's cavalry guarded Pantherskin Creek's crossings, north and east of Upperville. The night before, Pleasonton had received another brigade of Federal cavalry under Brig. Gen. William Averell, bringing his total force to nearly 4,000 men and 18 pieces of artillery. Stuart's line stretched thin to cover the several approaches that the Federals could take to Upperville. The 9th Virginia Cavalry, far to the west, guarded the Trappe Road while the 4th Virginia Cavalry watched the center near Kincheloe's Mill. The remainder of Stuart's cavalry waited near where modern-day Willisville Road crosses Pantherskin Creek.

For both sides, the objectives remained the same. Stuart had to delay the Federal advance as long as possible while Pleasonton had to push south as quickly as possible. Now, with his back against Ashby's Gap, Stuart had to be sure the Confederate infantry on the other side had cleared the gap on its march southward to Culpeper. To get all the Confederate infantry safely through the mountain gaps near Front Royal, Lee needed Stuart to delay the Federals

Recently put under local preservation easement, Vineyard Hill was a vital defensive position for Jeb Stuart in 1862. Stuart would find himself back in this same position in June 1863 during the Gettysburg Campaign, fending off Federal cavalry attacks. (rgmhaa)

one more day. Pleasonton, already delayed several crucial days, needed to push forward, clear the Loudoun Valley of the Confederate cavalry, and lead the Army of the Potomac's columns south to cut off the Confederate movement to Culpeper. By November 3, the Federal I Corps backed up on the roads north of Pleasonton's cavalry. Beyond that, the VI and IX Corps were north of Purcellville.

By 11:00 a.m., the brunt of Pleasonton's attack fell on Stuart's men near Willisville Road and Kincheloe's Mill. Pleasonton overestimated Stuart's force (a credit to Stuart's delaying tactics the previous couple of days) and advanced cautiously. Pleasonton ordered Averell's brigade to attack the Confederate center while his cavalry and Hoffman's infantry attacked the Confederates along Willisville Road. After a stubborn defense, Stuart's line began breaking east of Upperville. He ordered his men west along the turnpike to Upperville and Vineyard Hill. Here, he hoped to link up with the 4th Virginia Cavalry, which faced Averell's whole brigade but had yet to engage. However, this defensive line was not to be because Averell's men crossed Pantherskin Creek at 4:00 p.m. and forced the Virginians back. Outnumbered three to one and outfought, Stuart's cavalry and artillery raced through Upperville's streets, moving westward toward Ashby's Gap.

A small creek today, Pantherskin Creek runs through a valley that created a difficult military obstacle for Federal cavalry. (rgmhaa)

As Stuart's men fled for Ashby's Gap, Averell's cavalry quickly gave chase. At one point, it looked like the 9th Virginia Cavalry might be sacrificed to slow down the Federal pursuit, but soon artillery opened up above the hills west of Paris near Ashby's Gap. This was enough for the Federals to call off their pursuit. Since it was already near 5:00 p.m., the setting sun also assisted the Confederates. That night, Stuart held Ashby's Gap while the Federals encamped around Upperville. The next day Stuart pulled out of the gap, and the Union II Corps took possession. The Federal cavalry moved south toward Manassas Gap and then Chester Gap. By the time the Federals arrived, the Confederates had already moved safely through the gap. On November 5, Longstreet's corps arrived in Culpeper, and McClellan lost the race. After three days of fighting between nearly 5,000 men with an estimated 250 casualties, Jeb Stuart's cavalry sealed the fate of the Union commander.

Like Snicker's Gap, Ashby's Gap served as a major pass through the Blue Ridge Mountains. The gap was crucial in 1862 as it would give access to the Federals to attack the Confederate infantry retreating southward. Stuart had to hold off the Federal cavalry long enough for the Confederate infantry to clear the gap. Once they did, the Confederates would have the inside track to Culpeper, blocking McClellan from positioning himself astride the route to Richmond. (loc)

Make a right onto Route 50 East (John S. Mosby Highway), continue east for 3.7 miles, and make a right onto Route 713 (Rectors Lane). Then, make the immediate left onto Route 713 (Atoka Road). Travel for 5 miles and make a right onto Route 710 (Rectortown Road). Continue on Route 710 for 0.3 miles and make a left onto Route 713 (Maidstone Road). Travel for 0.5 miles, and spot the Civil War Trails marker on the left, in front of a nineteenth-century warehouse.

GPS: N 38.91617, W 77.86892

STOP 13: RECTORTOWN

This small farming community served as an important rail stop for local farmers to get their produce and wares to growing markets on the East Coast. On November 5, 1862, it became the epicenter of the Army of the Potomac as McClellan made his army headquarters near here. Ironically, at that same time President Abraham Lincoln wrote the orders that relieved McClellan from command of the Army of the Potomac. Lincoln, frustrated by McClellan's lack of aggressiveness after the battle of Antietam—not following Lee into Virginia and not blocking Lee's movement east toward Richmond—decided to remove McClellan and to promote Maj. Gen. Ambrose Burnside to

Today, Upperville maintains much of its historic and rural character. The town prospered upon the completion of the Ashy Gap Turnpike in 1810 (modern day Route 50). (rgmhaa)

command. Some historians have also argued the timing had political motives since McClellan's popularity rose within the Democratic Party. In the fall Congressional elections, Lincoln feared if he removed McClellan before the voting it could be used by the Democrats to gain more seats in Congress and derail his presidential war aims. Ultimately, Lincoln's frustrations with this general exceeded the boiling point. As he said to Francis Blair after making the decision, Lincoln had "tried long enough to bore with an auger too dull to take hold."

Arriving late on November 7 in a snowstorm, Brig. Gen. Catharinus Buckingham brought orders from Secretary of War Edwin Stanton to relieve McClellan. Buckingham's first stop was to see Burnside because if Burnside could not be convinced, then Buckingham must return to Washington rather than go on to McClellan. Buckingham delivered the orders to Burnside, who immediately rejected his new assignment. After more conversation and thought, Burnside realized that his refusal would not prevent McClellan's removal and that Burnside's rival, Joe Hooker, might receive command if Burnside passed on it. Thus, Burnside decided to accept the new post. However, he always lacked confidence in his fitness for the command role. The orders from Lincoln also removed Fitz John Porter from corps command. Porter, already under investigation for his actions at the battle of Second Manassas, was seen as a close ally of McClellan's.

Next, Burnside and Buckingham went to McClellan's tent where Buckingham issued the removal orders to McClellan. Reportedly, McClellan showed little emotion when he read the orders, and he immediately turned over command of the army to Burnside. McClellan soon wrote his wife, "They have made a great mistake. Alas for my poor country! I know in my inmost heart she never had a truer servant. I have informally turned over the command to Burnside, but shall go to-morrow to Warrenton with him, and perhaps remain a day or two there in order to give him all the information in my power . . . ."

The supposed location of McClellan's headquarters is on a hill on the west side of Lost Corner Road. To reach Lost Corner Road, take the road to the left of the Civil War Trails marker and safely cross the railroad tracks; this is Lost Corner Road. The several hills on the right side of the road ignite debate among local historians about which was the location of McClellan's headquarters tent. Lost Corner Road dead-ends in about 1.5 miles from the railroad crossing. To continue the tour, return to the Civil War Trails marker and pick up the directions below.

Brig. Gen. Catharinus Buckingham was a graduate of West Point in 1829 and excelled in mathematics and natural philosophy. In July 1862, he was promoted to brigadier general to serve as a special assistant to the Secretary of War. Buckingham had strict orders on what to do when he found McClellan's headquarters. (gliah)

From the parking area for the Civil War Trails marker, turn right onto Route 713 (Maidstone Road). Travel 0.5 miles and turn right to stay on Route 713, which now becomes Rectortown Road. In 4.4 miles, proceed straight through the traffic light onto US 17 Business S.

Local historians believe that this knoll was the headquarters of George McClellan when he was removed from command. (kp)

Secretary of War Edwin
Stanton became an influential
member of Lincoln's cabinet
and had grown tired of
McClellan's continued
defiance to civilian authority.
(loc)

On November 10, Maj. Gen.
Ambrose Burnside planned
a grand review of the Army
of the Potomac for the men
to see McClellan one last
time. Burnside convinced his
friend to remain in the area
for a few days to organize the
review. Burnside accompanied
McClellan as they rode
through miles of infantry lined
up for the occasion, several
miles north of Warrenton. (loc)

*In less than one mile, this becomes US 17 S. Continue
on US 17 S for 9.0 miles. Stay to the left to remain
on US 17 Business S (Broadview Avenue). Stay on
Broadview Avenue, which turns into Winchester Street.
Drive 1.1 miles and turn right onto Courthouse Square.
Make the next left onto Ashby Street. The Warren Green
Hotel is on your right. Street parking is limited so use the
nearby free public parking lots.*

GPS: N 38.71325, W 77.79587

STOP 14: WARRENTON-WARREN GREEN HOTEL

The Warren Green Hotel was one of the
finest hotels in Warrenton. Originally built as the
Norris Tavern in 1819, it hosted many national
dignitaries, such as the Marquis de Lafayette,
James Monroe, Henry Clay, Andrew Jackson, and
local partisan John Mosby. The reconstruction
now standing here was built after a fire destroyed
the original in 1876. It now serves as office space
for Fauquier County.

Learning about his dismissal, McClellan
wrote a farewell speech to the Army of the
Potomac during the evening of November 7. To
commemorate the occasion, the new commanding
general, Burnside, held a grand review of the
army north of Warrenton on November 10.
At the review, McClellan's speech was read to
the men who lined the road into Warrenton for
nearly three miles. As McClellan and Burnside
rode south into Warrenton, the army cheered
McClellan as a hero the entire way. The main
fear of Republicans in Congress and the Lincoln
administration stemmed from McClellan's
popularity with his men in the army, a popularity
giving rise to the idea that he could use this army
to launch a coup against the government. This
fear never materialized, but undoubtedly, the men
of the army loved their commander.

On November 11, a reception was held here
at the Warren Green Hotel for all the officers of
the Army of the Potomac. On the second-floor
balcony, McClellan issued his final farewell and
boarded a train bound for Washington, DC, and

then to Trenton, New Jersey, where he vainly awaited further orders from his country. With the removal of McClellan, the Maryland Campaign of 1862 ended, and a new chapter in the history of the Army of the Potomac began.

Today, this modern building is a rebuilt version of the original Warren Green Hotel, which burned in 1876. (kp)

McClellan was a man of fanfare, and his adieux to his officers at the Warren Green Hotel in Warrenton was one of many "farewells" given to McClellan. His popularity with his men and officers led many in the Lincoln administration to fear his power. He ended his farewell to his officers by saying, "Stand by General Burnside as you have stood by me, and all will be well." (hw)

Conclusion
CHAPTER SEVEN

When the smoke dissipated from the Maryland Campaign battlefields to reveal mangled corpses and destruction beyond one's imagination, many people searched for answers. Was all this worth it? And what did it mean? What had been gained or lost by the bloodiest single day in American history on the banks of the Antietam?

For Robert E. Lee and his Army of Northern Virginia, the campaign goals remained unaccomplished. Maryland refused to rip its star from the United States flag and sew it into the folds of the Confederacy. The army's stay in Maryland, much shorter than expected, failed to directly influence the fall elections in the North. Lee's desire to win another crushing victory over his enemy did not come to fruition. Foreign nations, most notably Britain, eyeing the campaign with keen interest, decided against conflict mediation. "History records few examples of greater fortitude and endurance than this army has exhibited," Lee extolled his soldiers. But "much as you have done, much more remains to be accomplished."

Robert E. Lee's foray into Maryland carried high the Confederate banner. A nation thought to be wilting away in the spring of 1862 now

President Andrew Johnson dedicated the Antietam National Cemetery in 1867, although the Private Soldier Monument in the center of the cemetery was not erected and dedicated until 1880. (kp)

Robert E. Lee knew how close he came to victory in Maryland. He tried for another war-ending victory in the North nine months later that culminated in another defeat for him—this time at the battle of Gettysburg. (loc)

perched its flag nearly on the Mason-Dixon Line in the east and the Ohio River in the west. Lee's Maryland Campaign tumbled down before him, and soon enough the Confederate advance across a thousand-mile front met similar setbacks at Perryville in Kentucky and Corinth in Mississippi. The Confederacy remained very much alive heading into the winter of 1862, but its best chance to achieve independence in one united movement slipped through its grasp.

For the United States, many of its citizens held bated breath as their Army of the Potomac grappled with the invading host in western Maryland. "There is a general feeling that the Southern Confederacy will be recognized & that they deserved to be recognized," wrote one Federal officer at the onset of the campaign. It seemed the country could not sustain itself through one more battlefield loss

in 1862. Fortunately, McClellan achieved his conservative goals: driving the enemy from the soil of the Old Line State and back into Virginia. A Union defeat did not happen in Maryland or anywhere in the rest of the country in the autumn of 1862.

Perhaps no one watched the campaign unfolding northwest of Washington City with greater anxiety than Abraham Lincoln. In early September, dissension amongst his Cabinet and the general reversal of the Federal war effort drove Lincoln into the darkest depths of melancholy. "[H]e felt almost ready to hang himself," recorded one Cabinet member. Like an invisible spirit over all of the marching, maneuvering, and fighting in Maryland hovered Lincoln's own decision earlier that summer to issue a proclamation of emancipation. Wait,

Confederate armies advanced across a one-thousand-mile front in the summer of 1862 but were turned back at Antietam; Corinth, Mississippi; and Perryville, Kentucky, pictured here. (loc)

Despite a shaky hand from greeting hundreds of visitors, Abraham Lincoln signed the Emancipation Proclamation into effect on New Year's Day 1863. "I never, in my life, felt more certain that I was doing right, than I do in signing this paper," he told onlookers to the momentous event. (loc)

his Secretary of State William Seward had told him, lest it look like the last desperate measure of a crumbling government. Lincoln waited longer than he wanted for a victory to buttress the announcement, but with the Confederate army out of Maryland, the President finally introduced this sweeping war measure. Five days after the battle of Antietam—two days after the end of the campaign—Lincoln called his Cabinet together and announced his decision.

The Maryland Campaign's conclusion and the September 22 announcement of the Preliminary Emancipation Proclamation signaled a significant shift in the war's trajectory. Confederates dug in their heels. "This will only intensify the war," said one. In Lincoln's eyes, this altered the course of the war and of the United States. "We must take a different path," he said. "The Administration must set the army an example, and strike at the heart of the rebellion."

Lee's Maryland Campaign and Lincoln's subsequent war-changing measure failed to end the Civil War, "but at Sharpsburg was sprung the keystone of the arch upon which the Confederate cause rested." September 1862 dawned as the Confederacy's best chance

African-Americans across North and South welcomed and cheered the Emancipation Proclamation on January 1, 1863. Lincoln's measure altered the course of the war and ratcheted up the stakes of its outcome. (loc)

to gain independence. Northern armies battled on, denying that opportunity while the slow, obscure downward spiral of Southern independence began on the backroads and open fields of western Maryland and northern Virginia.

The Emancipation Proclamation has appeared in many different forms since Lincoln signed it into law. This popularized and artistic version dates from 1888. (loc)

Suggested Reading

The Maryland Campaign of September 1862: Volumes I-III
Ezra Carman and Thomas G. Clemens (editor)
Savas Beatie (2010-2017)
ISBN: 9781932714814

Carman, a veteran of the campaign, produced the most detailed study of the campaign and battle. Clemens's edits and annotations add a new and worthwhile dimension to Carman's now-accessible manuscript.

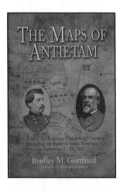

The Maps of Antietam: An Atlas of the Antietam (Sharpsburg) Campaign, including the Battle of South Mountain, September 2-20, 1862
Bradley M. Gottfried
Savas Beatie (2012)
ISBN: 9781611210866

Gottfried's foray into the Maryland Campaign provides an accessible and easy-to-follow narrative of the entire campaign with full color maps to take the reader step by step through the different maneuvers and battles.

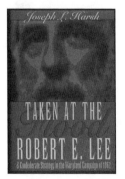

Taken at the Flood: Robert E. Lee and Confederate Strategy in the Maryland Campaign of 1862
Joseph L. Harsh
The Kent State University Press (1999)
ISBN: 9780873386319

Harsh's study of the Maryland Campaign cannot be ignored. His analysis of Robert E. Lee and the Confederate army in the campaign is fresh, insightful, and a good read.

To Antietam Creek: The Maryland Campaign of September 1862
D. Scott Hartwig
Johns Hopkins University Press (2012)
ISBN: 9781421406312

Hartwig's campaign study brings the armies only to the evening of September 16, 1862. It's a large undertaking but well worth the time to get through this balanced narrative.

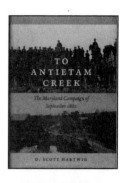

The Battle of South Mountain
John David Hoptak
The History Press (2011)
ISBN: 9781596294011

Hoptak provides a good look at the overlooked battle of South Mountain, fitting the battles at the mountain passes into the greater context of the campaign and Civil War.

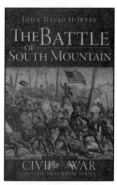

That Field of Blood: The Battle of Antietam, September 17, 1862
Daniel J. Vermilya
Savas Beatie (2018)
ISBN: 9781611213751

Vermilya, a former park ranger at Antietam, knows his subject incredibly well. His volume offers a reader-friendly focus on the battle of Antietam, loaded with maps and pictures of the battlefield.

About the Authors

Rob Orrison received his B.A. in Historic Preservation at Longwood College and received his M.A. in Public History from George Mason University. Rob has worked at various historic sites, museums and parks. Currently he serves as the Historic Site Operations Supervisor, overseeing day-to-day operations, programs and events of all Prince William County (VA) owned historic sites. Outside of work, Rob serves on the Board of Civil War Trails as the Northern Virginia Regional Director, board member of the Mosby Heritage Area Association, Treasurer of the Historic House Museum Consortium of Washington, D.C. and Vice President of the Virginia Association of Museums. His published works include *A Want of Vigilance: The Bristoe Station Campaign*; *The Last Road North: A Guide to the Gettysburg Campaign 1863*; and *A Single Blow: The Battles of Lexington and Concord and the Beginning of the American Revolution, April 19, 1775*. He lives in Dumfries, Virginia, with his wife Jamie and sons Carter and Grayson.

Kevin Pawlak is Director of Education for the Mosby Heritage Area Association and works as a Licensed Battlefield Guide at Antietam National Battlefield. He also sits on the Board of Directors of the Shepherdstown Battlefield Preservation Association and the Save Historic Antietam Foundation. Kevin serves on the advisory board at Shenandoah University's McCormick Civil War Institute and Shepherd University's George Tyler Moore Center for the Study of the Civil War. The History Press published his first book, *Shepherdstown in the Civil War: One Vast Confederate Hospital*, in 2015. He is a 2014 graduate of Shepherd University, where he received his B.A. in History with a concentration in Civil War and Nineteenth-Century America.

Rob and Kevin are both regular contributors to Emerging Civil War (www.emergingcivilwar.com).

EMERGING CIVIL WAR SERIES